Work Life Balance

ManageMentor Skill Pack

MANAGE ∎ MENTOR

BUSINESS MANAGEMENT

Lesson From,

Rebecca Knight, Mitchell Lee, Philip Mirvis, Ron Ashkenas, Vivien Corwin, Peter Frost, Katie Smith, Jenny Davis, Boris Groysberg, Clayton Christensen, Robert Quinn, Brianna Barker

Copyright © 2015 ManageMentor Business Management.
Nürnberg, Germany.

A CIP catalogue record for this title is available from the British
Library
ISBN: 1515051048

ISBN-13: 978-1515051046

Printed and bound by
Amazon Media EU S.à r.l. , 5 Rue Plaetis, L-2338 Luxemburg.

Amazon.com, Inc.; Seattle, WA 98108-1226, USA

CONTENTS

ACKNOWLEDGMENTS

- *Rebecca Knight* is a freelance journalist in Boston. She has been published in The New York Times, USA Today, The Financial Times, and The Economist.

- *Mitchell Lee Marks* is a leadership professor at San Francisco State University's College of Business and the president of JoiningForces.org.

- *Philip Mirvis* is an organizational psychologist and senior fellow at Boston College's Center for Corporate Citizenship.

- *Ron Ashkenas* is a managing partner of Schaffer Consulting. He is a co-author of *The GE Work-Out* and *The Boundaryless Organization*. His latest book is *Simply Effective*.

- *Vivien Corwin* is a consultant in leadership development and human resource management and an associate faculty member at Royal Roads University in Victoria, British Columbia.

- *Thomas B. Lawrence* is an associate professor at the University of Victoria's Faculty of Business.

- *Peter J. Frost* is the Edgar F. Kaiser Professor of Organizational Behavior at the University of British Columbia's Faculty of Commerce and Business Administration in Vancouver.

- *Katie Smith Milway* is a partner in Boston with The Bridgespan Group and former publisher at Bain & Company.

- *Ann Goggins Gregory* is Bridgespan's senior director of knowledge.

- *Jenny Davis-Peccoud* leads Bain & Company's Global Social Impact Practice, including the firm's externship program. She is also a senior director of the Global Organization practice.

- *Boris Groysberg* is a professor of business administration at Harvard Business School and the coauthor, with Robin Abrahams is a research associate at Harvard Business School.

- *Clayton M. Christensen* is a professor at Harvard Business School. He co-founded Innosight and Rose Park Advisors. He is the author of six books, including *The Innovator's Dilemma*.

- *Laura Morgan Roberts* is an assistant professor of organizational behavior at Harvard Business School in Boston.

- *Gretchen Spreitzer* is a professor of management and organizations at the University of Michigan's Ross School of Business.

- *Jane E. Dutton* is the Robert L. Kahn Distinguished University Professor of Business Administration and Psychology at the University of Michigan's Ross School of Business.

- *Robert E. Quinn* is the Margaret Elliott Tracy Collegiate Professor of Business Administration in the organization and management group at the University of Michigan's Ross School of Business in Ann Arbor.

- *Emily Heaphy* is a PhD candidate in management and organization at the Ross School of Business, and

- *Brianna Barker* is a PhD candidate in organizational psychology at the University of Michigan.

CHAPTER 1
How to Manage Oneself

Throughout history, people had little need to manage their careers—they were born into their stations in life or, in the recent past, they relied on their companies to chart their career paths. But times have drastically changed. Today we must all learn to manage ourselves.

What does that mean? As Peter Drucker tells us in this seminal article first published in 1999, it means we have to learn to develop ourselves. We have to place ourselves where we can make the greatest contribution to our organizations and communities. And we have to stay mentally alert and engaged during a 50-year working life, which means knowing how and when to change the work we do.

It may seem obvious that people achieve results by doing what they are good at and by working in ways that fit their abilities. But, Drucker says, very few people actually know—let alone take advantage of—their fundamental strengths.

He challenges each of us to ask ourselves: What are my strengths? How do I perform? What are my values? Where do I belong? What should my contribution be? Don't try to change yourself, Drucker cautions. Instead, concentrate on improving the skills you have and accepting assignments that are tailored to your individual way of working. If you do that, you can transform yourself from an ordinary worker into an outstanding performer.

Today's successful careers are not planned out in advance. They develop when people are prepared for opportunities because they have asked themselves those questions and have rigorously assessed their unique characteristics. This article challenges readers to take responsibility for managing their futures, both in and out of the office.

We live in an age of unprecedented opportunity: If you've got ambition and smarts, you can rise to the top of your chosen profession, regardless of where you started out.

But with opportunity comes responsibility. Companies today aren't managing their employees' careers; knowledge workers must, effectively, be their own chief executive officers. It's up to you to carve out your place, to know when to change course, and to keep yourself engaged and productive during a work life that may span some 50 years. To do those things well, you'll need to cultivate a deep understanding of yourself—not only what your strengths and weaknesses are but also how you learn, how you work with others, what your values are, and where you can make the greatest contribution. Because only when you operate from strengths can you achieve true excellence.

History's great achievers—a Napoléon, a da Vinci, a Mozart—have always managed themselves. That, in large measure, is what makes them great achievers. But they are rare exceptions, so unusual both in their talents and their accomplishments as to be considered outside the boundaries of ordinary human existence. Now, most of us, even those of us with modest endowments, will have to learn to manage ourselves. We will have to learn to develop ourselves. We will have to place ourselves where we can make the greatest contribution. And we will have to stay mentally alert and engaged during a 50-year working life, which means knowing how and when to change the work we do.

What Are My Strengths?

Most people think they know what they are good at. They are usually wrong. More often, people know what they are not good at and even then more people are wrong than right. And yet, a person can perform only from strength. One cannot build performance on weaknesses, let alone on something one cannot do at all.

Throughout history, people had little need to know their strengths. A person was born into a position and a line of work: The peasant's son would also be a peasant; the artisan's daughter, an artisan's wife; and so on. But now people have choices. We need to know our strengths in order to know where we belong.

The only way to discover your strengths is through feedback analysis. Whenever you make a key decision or take a key action, write down what you expect will happen. Nine or 12 months later, compare the actual results with your expectations. I have been practicing this method for 15 to 20 years now, and every time I do it, I am surprised. The feedback analysis showed me, for instance—and to my great surprise—that I have an intuitive understanding of technical people, whether they are engineers or accountants or market researchers. It also showed me that I don't really resonate with generalists.

Feedback analysis is by no means new. It was invented sometime in the fourteenth century by an otherwise totally obscure German theologian and picked up quite independently, some 150 years later, by John Calvin and Ignatius of Loyola, each of whom incorporated it into the practice of his followers. In fact, the steadfast focus on performance and results that this habit produces explains why the institutions these two men founded, the Calvinist church and the Jesuit order, came to dominate Europe within 30 years.

Practiced consistently, this simple method will show you within a fairly short period of time, maybe two or three years, where your strengths lie and this is the most important thing to know. The method will show you what you are doing or failing to do that deprives you of the full benefits of your strengths. It will show you where you are not particularly competent. And finally, it will show you where you have no strengths and cannot perform.

Several implications for action follow from feedback analysis. First and foremost, concentrate on your strengths. Put yourself where your strengths can produce results.

Second, work on improving your strengths. Analysis will rapidly show where you need to improve skills or acquire new ones. It will also show the gaps in your knowledge and those can usually be filled. Mathematicians are born, but everyone can learn trigonometry.

Third, discover where your intellectual arrogance is causing disabling ignorance and overcome it. Far too many people—especially people with great expertise in one area—are contemptuous of knowledge in other areas or believe that being bright is a substitute for knowledge. First-rate engineers, for instance, tend to take pride in not knowing anything about people. Human beings, they believe, are much too disorderly for the good engineering mind. Human resources professionals, by contrast, often pride themselves on their ignorance of elementary accounting or of quantitative methods altogether. But taking pride in such ignorance is self-defeating. Go to work on acquiring the skills and knowledge you need to fully realize your strengths.

It is equally essential to remedy your bad habits—the things you do or fail to do that inhibit your effectiveness and performance. Such habits will quickly show up in the feedback. For example, a planner may find that his beautiful plans fail because he does not follow through on them. Like so many brilliant people, he believes that ideas move mountains. But bulldozers move mountains; ideas show where the bulldozers should go to work. This planner will have to learn that the work does not stop when the plan is completed. He must find people to carry out the plan and explain it to them. He must adapt and change it as he puts it into action. And finally, he must decide when to stop pushing the plan.

At the same time, feedback will also reveal when the problem is a lack of manners. Manners are the lubricating oil of an organization. It is a law of nature that two moving bodies in contact with each other create friction. This is as true for human beings as it is for inanimate objects. Manners—simple things like saying "please" and "thank you" and knowing a person's name or asking after her family—enable two people to work together whether they like each other or not. Bright people, especially bright young people, often do not understand this. If analysis shows that someone's brilliant work fails again and again as soon as cooperation from others is required, it probably indicates a lack of courtesy—that is, a lack of manners.

Comparing your expectations with your results also indicates what not to do. We all have a vast number of areas in which we have no talent or skill and little chance of becoming even mediocre. In those areas a person—and especially a knowledge worker—should not take on work, jobs, and assignments. One should waste as little effort as possible on improving areas of low competence. It takes far more energy and work to improve from incompetence to mediocrity than it takes to improve from first-rate performance to excellence. And yet most people—especially most teachers and most organizations—concentrate on making incompetent performers into mediocre ones. Energy, resources, and time should go instead to making a competent person into a star performer.

It takes far more energy to improve from incompetence to mediocrity than to improve from first-rate performance to excellence.

How Do I Perform?

Amazingly few people know how they get things done. Indeed, most of us do not even know that different people work and perform differently. Too many people work in ways that are not their ways, and that almost guarantees nonperformance. For knowledge workers, How do I perform? may be an even more important question than What are my strengths?

Like one's strengths, how one performs is unique. It is a matter of personality. Whether personality be a matter of nature or nurture, it surely is formed long before a person goes to work. And *how* a person performs is a given, just as *what* a person is good at or not good at is a given. A person's way of performing can be slightly modified, but it is unlikely to be completely changed—and certainly not easily. Just as people achieve results by doing what they are good at, they also achieve results by working in ways that they best perform. A few common personality traits usually determine how a person performs.

Am I a reader or a listener?

The first thing to know is whether you are a reader or a listener. Far too few people even know that there are readers and listeners and that people are rarely both. Even fewer know which of the two they themselves are. But some examples will show how damaging such ignorance can be.

When Dwight Eisenhower was Supreme Commander of the Allied forces in Europe, he was the darling of the press. His press conferences were famous for their style—General Eisenhower showed total command of whatever question he was asked, and he was able to describe a situation and explain a policy in two or three beautifully polished and elegant sentences. Ten years later, the same journalists who had been his admirers held

President Eisenhower in open contempt. He never addressed the questions, they complained, but rambled on endlessly about something else. And they constantly ridiculed him for butchering the King's English in incoherent and ungrammatical answers.

Eisenhower apparently did not know that he was a reader, not a listener. When he was Supreme Commander in Europe, his aides made sure that every question from the press was presented in writing at least half an hour before a conference was to begin. And then Eisenhower was in total command. When he became president, he succeeded two listeners, Franklin D. Roosevelt and Harry Truman. Both men knew themselves to be listeners and both enjoyed free-for-all press conferences. Eisenhower may have felt that he had to do what his two predecessors had done. As a result, he never even heard the questions journalists asked. And Eisenhower is not even an extreme case of a nonlistener.

A few years later, Lyndon Johnson destroyed his presidency, in large measure, by not knowing that he was a listener. His predecessor, John Kennedy, was a reader who had assembled a brilliant group of writers as his assistants, making sure that they wrote to him before discussing their memos in person. Johnson kept these people on his staff—and they kept on writing. He never, apparently, understood one word of what they wrote. Yet as a senator, Johnson had been superb; for parliamentarians have to be, above all, listeners.

Few listeners can be made, or can make themselves, into competent readers and vice versa. The listener who tries to be a reader will, therefore, suffer the fate of Lyndon Johnson, whereas the reader who tries to be a listener will suffer the fate of Dwight Eisenhower. They will not perform or achieve.

How do I learn?

The second thing to know about how one performs is to know how one learns. Many first-class writers—Winston Churchill is but one example—do poorly in school. They tend to remember their schooling as pure torture. Yet few of their classmates remember it the same way. They may not have enjoyed the school very much, but the worst they suffered was boredom. The explanation is that writers do not, as a rule, learn by listening and reading. They learn by writing. Because schools do not allow them to learn this way, they get poor grades.

Schools everywhere are organized on the assumption that there is only one right way to learn and that it is the same way for everybody. But to be forced to learn the way a school teaches is sheer hell for students who learn differently. Indeed, there are probably half a dozen different ways to learn.

There are people, like Churchill, who learn by writing. Some people learn by taking copious notes. Beethoven, for example, left behind an enormous number of sketchbooks, yet he said he never actually looked at them when he composed. Asked why he kept them, he is reported to have replied, "If I don't write it down immediately, I forget it right away. If I put it into a sketchbook, I never forget it and I never have to look it up again." Some people learn by doing. Others learn by hearing themselves talk.

A chief executive I know who converted a small and mediocre family business into the leading company in its industry was one of those people who learn by talking. He was in the habit of calling his entire senior staff into his office once a week and then talking at them for two or three hours. He would raise policy issues and argue three different positions on each one. He rarely asked his associates for comments or questions; he simply needed an audience to hear himself talk. That's how he learned. And although he is a fairly extreme case, learning through talking is by no means an unusual method. Successful trial lawyers learn the same way, as do many medical diagnosticians (and so do I).

Of all the important pieces of self-knowledge, understanding how you learn is the easiest to acquire. When I ask people, "How do you learn?" most of them know the answer. But when I ask, "Do you act on this knowledge?" few answer yes. And yet, acting on this knowledge is the key to performance; or rather, *not* acting on this knowledge condemns one to nonperformance.

Am I a reader or a listener? and How do I learn? are the first questions to ask. But they are by no means the only ones. To manage yourself effectively, you also have to ask, Do I work well with people, or am I a loner? And if you do work well with people, you then must ask, In what relationship?

Some people work best as subordinates. General George Patton, the great American military hero of World War II, is a prime example. Patton was America's top troop commander. Yet when he was proposed for an independent command, General George Marshall, the U.S. chief of staff—and probably the most successful picker of men in U.S. history—said, "Patton is the best subordinate the American army has ever produced, but he would be the worst commander."

Some people work best as team members. Others work best alone. Some are exceptionally talented as coaches and mentors; others are simply incompetent as mentors.

Another crucial question is, Do I produce results as a decision maker or as an adviser? A great many people perform best as advisers but cannot take the burden and pressure of making the decision. A good many other people, by contrast, need an adviser to force themselves to think; then they can make decisions and act on them with speed, self-confidence, and courage.

This is a reason, by the way, that the number two person in an organization often fails when promoted to the number one position. The top spot requires a decision maker. Strong decision makers often put somebody they trust into the number two spot as their adviser and in that position the person is outstanding. But in the number one spot, the same person fails. He or she knows what the decision should be but cannot accept the responsibility of actually making it.

Other important questions to ask include, Do I perform well under stress, or do I need a highly structured and predictable environment? Do I work best in a big organization or a small one? Few people work well in all kinds of environments. Again and again, I have seen people who were very successful in large organizations flounder miserably when they moved into smaller ones. And the reverse is equally true.

The conclusion bears repeating: Do not try to change yourself—you are unlikely to succeed. But work hard to improve the way you perform. And try not to take on work you cannot perform or will only perform poorly.

Do not try to change yourself—you are unlikely to succeed. Work to improve the way you perform.

What Are My Values?

To be able to manage yourself, you finally have to ask, What are my values? This is not a question of ethics. With respect to ethics, the rules are the same for everybody, and the test is a simple one. I call it the "mirror test."

In the early years of this century, the most highly respected diplomat of all the great powers was the German ambassador in London. He was clearly destined for great things to become his country's foreign minister, at least, if not its federal chancellor. Yet in 1906 he abruptly resigned rather than preside over a dinner given by the diplomatic corps for Edward VII. The king was a notorious womanizer and made it clear what kind of dinner he wanted. The ambassador is reported to have said, "I refuse to see a pimp in the mirror in the morning when I shave."

That is the mirror test. Ethics requires that you ask yourself, What kind of person do I want to see in the mirror in the morning? What is ethical behavior in one kind of organization or situation is ethical behavior in another. But ethics is only part of a value system especially of an organization's value system.

To work in an organization whose value system is unacceptable or incompatible with one's own condemns a person both to frustration and to nonperformance.

Consider the experience of a highly successful human resources executive whose company was acquired by a bigger organization. After the acquisition, she was promoted to do the kind of work she did best, which included selecting people for important positions. The executive deeply believed that a company should hire people for such positions from the outside only after exhausting all the inside possibilities. But her new company believed in first looking outside "to bring in fresh blood." There is something to be said for both approaches—in my experience, the proper one is to do some of both. They are, however, fundamentally incompatible—not as policies but as values. They bespeak different views of the relationship between organizations and people; different views of the responsibility of an organization to its people and their development; and different views of a person's most important contribution to an enterprise. After several years of frustration, the executive quit—at considerable financial loss. Her values and the values of the organization simply were not compatible.

Similarly, whether a pharmaceutical company tries to obtain results by making constant, small improvements or by achieving occasional, highly expensive, and risky "breakthroughs" is not primarily an economic question. The results of either strategy may be pretty much the same. At bottom, there is a conflict between a value system that sees the company's contribution in terms of helping physicians do better what they already do and a value system that is oriented toward making scientific discoveries.

Whether a business should be run for short-term results or with a focus on the long term is likewise a question of values. Financial analysts believe that businesses can be run for both simultaneously. Successful businesspeople know better. To be sure, every company has to produce short-term results. But in any conflict between short-term results and long-term growth, each company will determine its own priority. This is not primarily a disagreement about economics. It is fundamentally a value conflict regarding the function of a business and the responsibility of management.

Value conflicts are not limited to business organizations. One of the fastest-growing pastoral churches in the United States measures success by the number of new parishioners. Its leadership believes that what matters is how many newcomers join the congregation. The Good Lord will then minister to their spiritual needs or at least to the needs of a sufficient percentage. Another pastoral, evangelical church believes that what matters is people's spiritual growth. The church eases out newcomers who join but do not enter into its spiritual life.

Again, this is not a matter of numbers. At first glance, it appears that the second church grows more slowly. But it retains a far larger proportion of newcomers than the first one does. Its growth, in other words, is more solid. This is also not a theological problem, or only secondarily so. It is a problem about values. In a public debate, one pastor argued, "Unless you first come to church, you will never find the gate to the Kingdom of Heaven."

"No," answered the other. "Until you first look for the gate to the Kingdom of Heaven, you don't belong in church."

Organizations, like people, have values. To be effective in an organization, a person's values must be compatible with the organization's values. They do not need to be the same, but they must be close enough to coexist. Otherwise, the person will not only be frustrated but also will not produce results.

A person's strengths and the way that person performs rarely conflict; the two are complementary. But there is sometimes a conflict between a person's values and his or her strengths. What one does well—even very well and successfully—may not fit with one's value system. In that case, the work may not appear to be worth devoting one's life to (or even a substantial portion thereof).

What one does well—even very well and successfully—may not fit with one's value system. If I may, allow me to interject a personal note. Many years ago, I too had to decide between my values and what I was doing successfully. I was doing very well as a young investment banker in London in the mid-1930s, and the work clearly fit my strengths. Yet I did not see myself making a contribution as an asset manager. People, I realized, were what I valued, and I saw no point in being the richest man in the cemetery. I had no money and no other job prospects. Despite the continuing Depression, I quit—and it was the right thing to do. Values, in other words, are and should be the ultimate test.

Where Do I Belong?

A small number of people know very early where they belong. Mathematicians, musicians, and cooks, for instance, are usually mathematicians, musicians, and cooks by the time they are four or five years old. Physicians usually decide on their careers in their teens, if not earlier. But most people, especially highly gifted people, do not really know where they belong until they are well past their mid-twenties. By that time, however, they should know the answers to the three questions: What are my strengths? How do I perform? and, What are my values? And then they can and should decide where they belong.

Or rather, they should be able to decide where they do *not* belong. The person who has learned that he or she does not perform well in a big organization should have learned to say no to a position in one. The person who has learned that he or she is not a decision maker should have learned to say no to a decision-making assignment. A General Patton (who probably never learned this himself) should have learned to say no to an independent command.

Equally important, knowing the answer to these questions enables a person to say to an opportunity, an offer, or an assignment, "Yes, I will do that. But this is the way I should be doing it. This is the way it should be structured. This is the way the relationships should be. These are the kind of results you should expect from me, and in this time frame, because this is who I am."

Successful careers are not planned. They develop when people are prepared for opportunities because they know their strengths, their method of work, and their values. Knowing where one belongs can transform an ordinary person—hardworking and competent but otherwise mediocre into an outstanding performer.

What Should I Contribute?

Throughout history, the great majority of people never had to ask the question, What should I contribute? They were told what to contribute, and their tasks were dictated either by the work itself—as it was for the peasant or artisan—or by a master or a mistress—as it was for domestic servants. And until very recently, it was taken for granted that most people were subordinates who did as they were told. Even in the 1950s and 1960s, the new knowledge workers (the so-called organization men) looked to their company's personnel department to plan their careers.

Then in the late 1960s, no one wanted to be told what to do any longer. Young men and women began to ask, What do *I* want to do? And what they heard was that the way to contribute was to "do your own thing." But this solution was as wrong as the organization men's had been. Very few of the people who believed that doing one's own thing would lead to contribution, self-fulfillment, and success achieved any of the three.

But still, there is no return to the old answer of doing what you are told or assigned to do. Knowledge workers in particular have to learn to ask a question that has not been asked before: What *should* my contribution be? To answer it, they must address three distinct elements: What does the situation require? Given my strengths, my way of performing, and my values, how can I make the greatest contribution to what needs to be done? And finally, What results have to be achieved to make a difference?

Consider the experience of a newly appointed hospital administrator. The hospital was big and prestigious, but it had been coasting on its reputation for 30 years. The new administrator decided that his contribution should be to establish a standard of excellence in one important area within two years. He chose to focus on the emergency room, which was big, visible, and sloppy. He decided that every patient who came into the ER had to be seen by a qualified nurse within 60 seconds. Within 12 months, the hospital's emergency room had become a model for all hospitals in the United States, and within another two years, the whole hospital had been transformed.

As this example suggests, it is rarely possible—or even particularly fruitful—to look too far ahead. A plan can usually cover no more than 18 months and still be reasonably clear and specific. So the question in most cases should be, Where and how can I achieve results that will make a difference within the next year and a half? The answer must balance several things. First, the results should be hard to achieve—they should require "stretching," to use the current buzzword. But also, they should be within reach. To aim at results that cannot be achieved—or that can be only under the most unlikely circumstances is not being ambitious; it is being foolish. Second, the results should be meaningful. They should make a difference. Finally, results should be visible and, if at all possible, measurable. From this will come a course of action: what to do, where and how to start, and what goals and deadlines to set.

Responsibility for Relationships

Very few people work by themselves and achieve results by themselves—a few great artists, a few great scientists, a few great athletes. Most people work with others and are effective with other people. That is true whether they are members of an organization or independently employed. Managing yourself requires taking responsibility for relationships. This has two parts.

The first is to accept the fact that other people are as much individuals as you yourself are. They perversely insist on behaving like human beings. This means that they too have their strengths; they too have their ways of getting things done; they too have their values. To be effective, therefore, you have to know the strengths, the performance modes, and the values of your coworkers.

That sounds obvious, but few people pay attention to it. Typical is the person who was trained to write reports in his or her first assignment because that boss was a reader. Even if the next boss is a listener, the person goes on writing reports that, invariably, produce no results. Invariably the boss will think the employee is stupid, incompetent, and lazy, and he or she will fail. But that could have been avoided if the employee had only looked at the new boss and analyzed how *this* boss performs.

Bosses are neither a title on the organization chart nor a "function." They are individuals and are entitled to do their work in the way they do it best. It is incumbent on the people who work with them to observe them, to find out how they work, and to adapt themselves to what makes their bosses most effective. This, in fact, is the secret of "managing" the boss.

The same holds true for all your coworkers. Each works his or her way, not your way. And each is entitled to work in his or her way. What matters is whether they perform and what their values are. As for how they perform—each is likely to do it differently. The first secret of effectiveness is to understand the people you work with and depend on so that you can make use of their strengths, their ways of working, and their values. Working relationships are as much based on the people as they are on the work.

The first secret of effectiveness is to understand the people you work with so that you can make use of their strengths.

The second part of relationship responsibility is taking responsibility for communication. Whenever I, or any other consultant, start to work with an organization, the first thing I hear about are all the personality conflicts. Most of these arise from the fact that people do not know what other people are doing and how they do their work, or what contribution the other people are concentrating on and what results they expect. And the reason they do not know is that they have not asked and therefore have not been told.

This failure to ask reflects human stupidity less than it reflects human history. Until recently, it was unnecessary to tell any of these things to anybody. In the medieval city, everyone in a district plied the same trade. In the countryside, everyone in a valley planted the same crop as soon as the frost was out of the ground. Even those few people who did things that were not "common" worked alone, so they did not have to tell anyone what they were doing.

Today the great majority of people work with others who have different tasks and responsibilities. The marketing vice president may have come out of sales and know everything about sales, but she knows nothing about the things she has never done—pricing, advertising, packaging, and the like. So the people who do these things must make sure that the marketing vice president understands what they are trying to do, why they are trying to do it, how they are going to do it, and what results to expect.

If the marketing vice president does not understand what these high-grade knowledge specialists are doing, it is primarily their fault, not hers. They have not educated her. Conversely, it is the marketing vice president's responsibility to make sure that all of her coworkers understand how she looks at marketing: what her goals are, how she works, and what she expects of herself and of each one of them.

Even people who understand the importance of taking responsibility for relationships often do not communicate sufficiently with their associates. They are afraid of being thought presumptuous or inquisitive or stupid. They are wrong. Whenever someone goes to his or her associates and says,

"This is what I am good at. This is how I work. These are my values. This is the contribution I plan to concentrate on and the results I should be expected to deliver," the response is always, "This is most helpful. But why didn't you tell me earlier?"

And one gets the same reaction without exception, in my experience—if one continues by asking, "And what do I need to know about your strengths, how you perform, your values, and your proposed contribution?" In fact, knowledge workers should request this of everyone with whom they work, whether as subordinate, superior, colleague, or team member. And again, whenever this is done, the reaction is always, "Thanks for asking me. But why didn't you ask me earlier?"

Organizations are no longer built on force but on trust. The existence of trust between people does not necessarily mean that they like one another. It means that they understand one another. Taking responsibility for relationships is therefore an absolute necessity. It is a duty. Whether one is a member of the organization, a consultant to it, a supplier, or a distributor, one owes that responsibility to all one's coworkers: those whose work one depends on as well as those who depend on one's own work.

The Second Half of Your Life

When work for most people meant manual labor, there was no need to worry about the second half of your life. You simply kept on doing what you had always done. And if you were lucky enough to survive 40 years of hard work in the mill or on the railroad, you were quite happy to spend the rest of your life doing nothing. Today, however, most work is knowledge work, and knowledge workers are not "finished" after 40 years on the job, they are merely bored.

We hear a great deal of talk about the midlife crisis of the executive. It is mostly boredom. At 45, most executives have reached the peak of their business careers, and they know it. After 20 years of doing very much the same kind of work, they are very good at their jobs. But they are not learning or contributing or deriving challenge and satisfaction from the job. And yet they are still likely to face another 20 if not 25 years of work. That is why managing oneself increasingly leads one to begin a second career.

There are three ways to develop a second career. The first is actually to start one. Often this takes nothing more than moving from one kind of organization to another: the divisional controller in a large corporation, for instance, becomes the controller of a medium-sized hospital. But there are also growing numbers of people who move into different lines of work altogether: the business executive or government official who enters the ministry at 45, for instance; or the midlevel manager who leaves corporate life after 20 years to attend law school and become a small-town attorney.

We will see many more second careers undertaken by people who have achieved modest success in their first jobs. Such people have substantial skills, and they know how to work. They need a community—the house is empty with the children gone and they need income as well. But above all, they need challenge.

The second way to prepare for the second half of your life is to develop a parallel career. Many people who are very successful in their first careers stay in the work they have been doing, either on a full-time or part-time or consulting basis. But in addition, they create a parallel job, usually in a nonprofit organization, that takes another ten hours of work a week. They might take over the administration of their church, for instance, or the presidency of the local Girl Scouts council. They might run the battered women's shelter, work as a children's librarian for the local public library, sit on the school board, and so on.

Finally, there are the social entrepreneurs. These are usually people who have been very successful in their first careers. They love their work, but it no longer challenges them. In many cases they keep on doing what they have been doing all along but spend less and less of their time on it. They also start another activity, usually a nonprofit. My friend Bob Buford, for example, built a very successful television company that he still runs. But he has also founded and built a successful nonprofit organization that works with Protestant churches, and he is building another to teach social entrepreneurs how to manage their own nonprofit ventures while still running their original businesses.

People who manage the second half of their lives may always be a minority. The majority may "retire on the job" and count the years until their actual retirement. But it is this minority, the men and women who see a long working-life expectancy as an opportunity both for themselves and for society, who will become leaders and models.

There is one prerequisite for managing the second half of your life: You must begin long before you enter it. When it first became clear 30 years ago that working-life expectancies were lengthening very fast, many observers (including myself) believed that retired people would increasingly become volunteers for nonprofit institutions. That has not happened. If one does not begin to volunteer before one is 40 or so, one will not volunteer once past 60.

There is one prerequisite for managing the second half of your life: You must begin doing so long before you enter it.

Similarly, all the social entrepreneurs I know began to work in their chosen second enterprise long before they reached their peak in their original business. Consider the example of a successful lawyer, the legal counsel to a large corporation, who has started a venture to establish model schools in his state. He began to do volunteer legal work for the schools when he was around 35. He was elected to the school board at age 40. At age 50, when he had amassed a fortune, he started his own enterprise to build and to run model schools. He is, however, still working nearly full-time as the lead counsel in the company he helped found as a young lawyer.

There is another reason to develop a second major interest, and to develop it early. No one can expect to live very long without experiencing a serious setback in his or her life or work. There is the competent engineer who is passed over for promotion at age 45. There is the competent college professor who realizes at age 42 that she will never get a professorship at a big university, even though she may be fully qualified for it. There are tragedies in one's family life: the breakup of one's marriage or the loss of a child. At such times, a second major interest—not just a hobby—may make all the difference. The engineer, for example, now knows that he has not been very successful in his job. But in his outside activity as church treasurer, for example—he is a success. One's family may break up, but in that outside activity there is still a community.

In a society in which success has become so terribly important, having options will become increasingly vital. Historically, there was no such thing as "success." The overwhelming majority of people did not expect anything but to stay in their "proper station," as an old English prayer has it. The only mobility was downward mobility.

In a knowledge society, however, we expect everyone to be a success. This is clearly an impossibility. For a great many people, there is at best an absence of failure. Wherever there is success, there has to be failure. And then it is vitally important for the individual, and equally for the individual's family, to have an area in which he or she can contribute, make a difference, and be *somebody*. That means finding a second area whether in a second career, a parallel career, or a social venture that offers an opportunity for being a leader, for being respected, for being a success.

The challenges of managing oneself may seem obvious, if not elementary. And the answers may seem self-evident to the point of appearing naïve. But managing oneself requires new and unprecedented things from the individual, and especially from the knowledge worker. In effect, managing oneself demands that each knowledge worker think and behave like a chief executive officer. Further, the shift from manual workers who do as they are told to knowledge workers who have to manage themselves profoundly challenges social structure. Every existing society, even the most individualistic one, takes two things for granted, if only subconsciously: that organizations outlive workers, and that most people stay put.

But today the opposite is true. Knowledge workers outlive organizations, and they are mobile. The need to manage oneself is therefore creating a revolution in human affairs.

CHAPTER 2

How Will You Measure Your Life?

Harvard Business School's Christensen teaches aspiring MBAs how to apply management and innovation theories to build stronger companies. But he also believes that these models can help people lead better lives. In this article, he explains how, exploring questions everyone needs to ask: How can I be happy in my career? How can I be sure that my relationship with my family is an enduring source of happiness? And how can I live my life with integrity?

The answer to the first question comes from Frederick Herzberg's assertion that the most powerful motivator isn't money; it's the opportunity to learn, grow in responsibilities, contribute, and be recognized. That's why management, if practiced well, can be the noblest of occupations; no others offer as many ways to help people find those opportunities. It isn't about buying, selling, and investing in companies, as many think.

The principles of resource allocation can help people attain happiness at home. If not managed masterfully, what emerges from a firm's resource allocation process can be very different from the strategy management intended to follow. That's true in life too: If you're not guided by a clear sense of purpose, you're likely to fritter away your time and energy on obtaining the most tangible, short-term signs of achievement, not what's really important to you.

And just as a focus on marginal costs can cause bad corporate decisions, it can lead people astray. The marginal cost of doing something wrong "just this once" always seems alluringly low. You don't see the end result to which that path leads. The key is to define what you stand for and draw the line in a safe place.

Before I published *The Innovator's Dilemma*, I got a call from Andrew Grove, then the chairman of Intel. He had read one of my early papers about disruptive technology, and he asked if I could talk to his direct reports and explain my research and what it implied for Intel. Excited, I flew to Silicon Valley and showed up at the appointed time, only to have Grove say, "Look, stuff has happened. We have only 10 minutes for you. Tell us what your model of disruption means for Intel." I said that I couldn't—that I needed a full 30 minutes to explain the model, because only with it as context would any comments about Intel make sense. Ten minutes into my explanation, Grove interrupted: "Look, I've got your model. Just tell us what it means for Intel."

I insisted that I needed 10 more minutes to describe how the process of disruption had worked its way through a very different industry, steel, so that he and his team could understand how disruption worked. I told the story of how Nucor and other steel minimills had begun by attacking the lowest end of the market—steel reinforcing bars, or rebar—and later moved up toward the high end, undercutting the traditional steel mills.

When I finished the minimill story, Grove said, "OK, I get it. What it means for Intel is...," and then went on to articulate what would become the company's strategy for going to the bottom of the market to launch the Celeron processor.

I've thought about that a million times since. If I had been suckered into telling Andy Grove what he should think about the microprocessor business, I'd have been killed. But instead of telling him what to think, I taught him how to think—and then he reached what I felt was the correct decision on his own.

That experience had a profound influence on me. When people ask what I think they should do, I rarely answer their question directly. Instead, I run the question aloud through one of my models. I'll describe how the process in the model worked its way through an industry quite different from their own. And then, more often than not, they'll say, "OK, I get it." And they'll answer their own question more insightfully than I could have.

My class at HBS is structured to help my students understand what good management theory is and how it is built. To that backbone I attach different models or theories that help students think about the various dimensions of a general manager's job in stimulating innovation and growth. In each session we look at one company through the lenses of those theories—using them to explain how the company got into its situation and to examine what managerial actions will yield the needed results.

On the last day of class, I ask my students to turn those theoretical lenses on themselves, to find cogent answers to three questions: First, how can I be sure that I'll be happy in my career? Second, how can I be sure that my relationships with my spouse and my family become an enduring source of happiness? Third, how can I be sure I'll stay out of jail? Though the last question sounds lighthearted, it's not. Two of the 32 people in my Rhodes scholar class spent time in jail. Jeff Skilling of Enron fame was a classmate of mine at HBS. These were good guys—but something in their lives sent them off in the wrong direction.

The Class of 2010

"I came to business school knowing exactly what I wanted to do—and I'm leaving choosing the exact opposite. I've worked in the private sector all my life, because everyone always told me that's where smart people are. But I've decided to try government and see if I can find more meaning there. "I used to think that industry was very safe. The recession has shown us that nothing is safe."

Ruhana Hafiz,Harvard Business School, Class of 2010

Her Plans: To join the FBI as a special adviser (a management track position)

"You could see a shift happening at HBS. Money used to be number one in the job search. When you make a ton of money, you want more of it. Ironic thing. You start to forget what the drivers of happiness are and what things are really important. A lot of people on campus see money differently now. They think, 'What's the minimum I need to have, and what else drives my life?' instead of 'What's the place where I can get the maximum of both?'"

Patrick Chun,Harvard Business School, Class of 2010

His Plans: To join Bain Capital

"The financial crisis helped me realize that you have to do what you really love in life. My current vision of success is based on the impact I can have, the experiences I can gain, and the happiness I can find personally, much more so than the pursuit of money or prestige. My main motivations are (1) to be with my family and people I care about; (2) to do something fun, exciting, and impactful; and (3) to pursue a long-term career in entrepreneurship, where I can build companies that change the way the world works."

Matt Salzberg,Harvard Business School, Class of 2010

His Plans: To work for Bessemer Venture Partners

"Because I'm returning to McKinsey, it probably seems like not all that much has changed for me. But while I was at HBS, I decided to do the dual degree at the Kennedy School. With the elections in 2008 and the economy looking shaky, it seemed more compelling for me to get a better understanding of the public and nonprofit sectors. In a way, that drove my return to McKinsey, where I'll have the ability to explore private, public, and nonprofit sectors.

"The recession has made us step back and take stock of how lucky we are. The crisis to us is 'Are we going to have a job by April?' Crisis to a lot of people is 'Are we going to stay in our home?'"

John Coleman,Harvard Business School, Class of 2010

His Plans: To return to McKinsey & Company

As the students discuss the answers to these questions, I open my own life to them as a case study of sorts, to illustrate how they can use the theories from our course to guide their life decisions.

One of the theories that gives great insight on the first question—how to be sure we find happiness in our careers—is from Frederick Herzberg, who asserts that the powerful motivator in our lives isn't money; it's the opportunity to learn, grow in responsibilities, contribute to others, and be recognized for achievements. I tell the students about a vision of sorts I had while I was running the company I founded before becoming an academic. In my mind's eye I saw one of my managers leave for work one morning with a relatively strong level of self-esteem. Then I pictured her driving home to her family 10 hours later, feeling unappreciated, frustrated, underutilized, and demeaned. I imagined how profoundly her lowered self-esteem affected the way she interacted with her children. The vision in my mind then fast-forwarded to another day, when she drove home with greater self-esteem—feeling that she had learned a lot, been recognized for achieving valuable things, and played a significant role in the success of some important initiatives. I then imagined how positively that affected her as a spouse and a parent. My conclusion: Management is the most noble of professions if it's practiced well. No other occupation offers as many ways to help others learn and grow, take responsibility and be recognized for achievement, and contribute to the success of a team. More and more MBA students come to school thinking that a career in business means buying, selling, and investing in companies. That's unfortunate. Doing deals doesn't yield the deep rewards that come from building up people.

Doing deals doesn't yield the deep rewards that come from building up people.

I want students to leave my classroom knowing that.

Create a Strategy for Your Life

A theory that is helpful in answering the second question—How can I ensure that my relationship with my family proves to be an enduring source of happiness?—concerns how strategy is defined and implemented. Its primary insight is that a company's strategy is determined by the types of initiatives that management invests in. If a company's resource allocation process is not managed masterfully, what emerges from it can be very different from what management intended. Because companies' decision-making systems are designed to steer investments to initiatives that offer the most tangible and immediate returns, companies shortchange investments in initiatives that are crucial to their long-term strategies.

Over the years I've watched the fates of my HBS classmates from 1979 unfold; I've seen more and more of them come to reunions unhappy, divorced, and alienated from their children. I can guarantee you that not a single one of them graduated with the deliberate strategy of getting divorced and raising children who would become estranged from them. And yet a shocking number of them implemented that strategy. The reason? They didn't keep the purpose of their lives front and center as they decided how to spend their time, talents, and energy.

It's quite startling that a significant fraction of the 900 students that HBS draws each year from the world's best have given little thought to the purpose of their lives. I tell the students that HBS might be one of their last chances to reflect deeply on that question. If they think that they'll have more time and energy to reflect later, they're nuts, because life only gets more demanding: You take on a mortgage; you're working 70 hours a week; you have a spouse and children.

For me, having a clear purpose in my life has been essential. But it was something I had to think long and hard about before I understood it. When I was a Rhodes scholar, I was in a very demanding academic program, trying to cram an extra year's worth of work into my time at Oxford. I decided to spend an hour every night reading, thinking, and praying about why God put me on this earth. That was a very challenging commitment to keep, because every hour I spent doing that, I wasn't studying applied econometrics. I was conflicted about whether I could really afford to take that time away from my studies, but I stuck with it—and ultimately figured out the purpose of my life.

Had I instead spent that hour each day learning the latest techniques for mastering the problems of autocorrelation in regression analysis, I would have badly misspent my life. I apply the tools of econometrics a few times a year, but I apply my knowledge of the purpose of my life every day. It's the single most useful thing I've ever learned. I promise my students that if they take the time to figure out their life purpose, they'll look back on it as the most important thing they discovered at HBS. If they don't figure it out, they will just sail off without a rudder and get buffeted in the very rough seas of life. Clarity about their purpose will trump knowledge of activity-based costing, balanced scorecards, core competence, disruptive innovation, the four Ps, and the five forces.

My purpose grew out of my religious faith, but faith isn't the only thing that gives people direction. For example, one of my former students decided that his purpose was to bring honesty and economic prosperity to his country and to raise children who were as capably committed to this cause, and to each other, as he was. His purpose is focused on family and others as mine is.

The choice and successful pursuit of a profession is but one tool for achieving your purpose. But without a purpose, life can become hollow.

Allocate Your Resources

Your decisions about allocating your personal time, energy, and talent ultimately shape your life's strategy.

21

I have a bunch of "businesses" that compete for these resources: I'm trying to have a rewarding relationship with my wife, raise great kids, contribute to my community, succeed in my career, contribute to my church, and so on. And I have exactly the same problem that a corporation does. I have a limited amount of time and energy and talent. How much do I devote to each of these pursuits?

Allocation choices can make your life turn out to be very different from what you intended. Sometimes that's good: Opportunities that you never planned for emerge. But if you misinvest your resources, the outcome can be bad. As I think about my former classmates who inadvertently invested for lives of hollow unhappiness, I can't help believing that their troubles relate right back to a short-term perspective.

When people who have a high need for achievement—and that includes all Harvard Business School graduates—have an extra half hour of time or an extra ounce of energy, they'll unconsciously allocate it to activities that yield the most tangible accomplishments. And our careers provide the most concrete evidence that we're moving forward. You ship a product, finish a design, complete a presentation, close a sale, teach a class, publish a paper, get paid, get promoted. In contrast, investing time and energy in your relationship with your spouse and children typically doesn't offer that same immediate sense of achievement. Kids misbehave every day. It's really not until 20 years down the road that you can put your hands on your hips and say, "I raised a good son or a good daughter." You can neglect your relationship with your spouse, and on a day-to-day basis, it doesn't seem as if things are deteriorating. People who are driven to excel have this unconscious propensity to underinvest in their families and overinvest in their careers—even though intimate and loving relationships with their families are the most powerful and enduring source of happiness.

If you study the root causes of business disasters, over and over you'll find this predisposition toward endeavors that offer immediate gratification. If you look at personal lives through that lens, you'll see the same stunning and sobering pattern: people allocating fewer and fewer resources to the things they would have once said mattered most.

Create a Culture

There's an important model in our class called the Tools of Cooperation, which basically says that being a visionary manager isn't all it's cracked up to be. It's one thing to see into the foggy future with acuity and chart the course corrections that the company must make. But it's quite another to persuade employees who might not see the changes ahead to line up and work cooperatively to take the company in that new direction. Knowing what tools to wield to elicit the needed cooperation is a critical managerial skill.

The theory arrays these tools along two dimensions—the extent to which members of the organization agree on what they want from their participation in the enterprise, and the extent to which they agree on what actions will produce the desired results. When there is little agreement on both axes, you have to use "power tools"—coercion, threats, punishment, and so on—to secure cooperation. Many companies start in this quadrant, which is why the founding executive team must play such an assertive role in defining what must be done and how. If employees' ways of working together to address those tasks succeed over and over, consensus begins to form.

MIT's Edgar Schein has described this process as the mechanism by which a culture is built. Ultimately, people don't even think about whether their way of doing things yields success. They embrace priorities and follow procedures by instinct and assumption rather than by explicit decision which means that they've created a culture. Culture, in compelling but unspoken ways, dictates the proven, acceptable methods by which members of the group address recurrent problems. And culture defines the priority given to different types of problems. It can be a powerful management tool.

In using this model to address the question, How can I be sure that my family becomes an enduring source of happiness?, my students quickly see that the simplest tools that parents can wield to elicit cooperation from children are power tools. But there comes a point during the teen years when power tools no longer work. At that point parents start wishing that they had begun working with their children at a very young age to build a culture at home in which children instinctively behave respectfully toward one another, obey their parents, and choose the right thing to do. Families have cultures, just as companies do. Those cultures can be built consciously or evolve inadvertently.

If you want your kids to have strong self-esteem and confidence that they can solve hard problems, those qualities won't magically materialize in high school. You have to design them into your family's culture and you have to think about this very early on. Like employees, children build self-esteem by doing things that are hard and learning what works.

Avoid the "Marginal Costs" Mistake

We're taught in finance and economics that in evaluating alternative investments, we should ignore sunk and fixed costs, and instead base decisions on the marginal costs and marginal revenues that each alternative entails. We learn in our course that this doctrine biases companies to leverage what they have put in place to succeed in the past, instead of guiding them to create the capabilities they'll need in the future. If we knew the future would be exactly the same as the past, that approach would be fine. But if the future's different—and it almost always is—then it's the wrong thing to do.

This theory addresses the third question I discuss with my students—how to live a life of integrity (stay out of jail). Unconsciously, we often employ the marginal cost doctrine in our personal lives when we choose between right and wrong. A voice in our head says, "Look, I know that as a general rule, most people shouldn't do this. But in this particular extenuating circumstance, just this once, it's OK." The marginal cost of doing something wrong "just this once" always seems alluringly low. It suckers you in, and you don't ever look at where that path ultimately is headed and at the full costs that the choice entails. Justification for infidelity and dishonesty in all their manifestations lies in the marginal cost economics of "just this once."

I'd like to share a story about how I came to understand the potential damage of "just this once" in my own life. I played on the Oxford University varsity basketball team. We worked our tails off and finished the season undefeated. The guys on the team were the best friends I've ever had in my life. We got to the British equivalent of the NCAA tournament and made it to the final four. It turned out the championship game was scheduled to be played on a Sunday. I had made a personal commitment to God at age 16 that I would never play ball on Sunday. So I went to the coach and explained my problem. He was incredulous. My teammates were, too, because I was the starting center. Every one of the guys on the team came to me and said, "You've got to play. Can't you break the rule just this one time?"

I'm a deeply religious man, so I went away and prayed about what I should do. I got a very clear feeling that I shouldn't break my commitment—so I didn't play in the championship game.

In many ways that was a small decision—involving one of several thousand Sundays in my life. In theory, surely I could have crossed over the line just that one time and then not done it again. But looking back on it, resisting the temptation whose logic was "In this extenuating circumstance, just this once, it's OK" has proven to be one of the most important decisions of my life. Why? My life has been one unending stream of extenuating circumstances. Had I crossed the line that one time, I would have done it over and over in the years that followed.

The lesson I learned from this is that it's easier to hold to your principles 100% of the time than it is to hold to them 98% of the time. If you give in to "just this once," based on a marginal cost analysis, as some of my former classmates have done, you'll regret where you end up. You've got to define for yourself what you stand for and draw the line in a safe place.

Remember the Importance of Humility

I got this insight when I was asked to teach a class on humility at Harvard College. I asked all the students to describe the most humble person they knew. One characteristic of these humble people stood out: They had a high level of self-esteem. They knew who they were, and they felt good about who they were. We also decided that humility was defined not by self-deprecating behavior or attitudes but by the esteem with which you regard others. Good behavior flows naturally from that kind of humility. For example, you would never steal from someone, because you respect that person too much. You'd never lie to someone, either.

It's crucial to take a sense of humility into the world. By the time you make it to a top graduate school, almost all your learning has come from people who are smarter and more experienced than you: parents, teachers, bosses. But once you've finished at Harvard Business School or any other top academic institution, the vast majority of people you'll interact with on a day-to-day basis may not be smarter than you. And if your attitude is that only smarter people have something to teach you, your learning opportunities will be very limited. But if you have a humble eagerness to learn something from everybody, your learning opportunities will be unlimited. Generally, you can be humble only if you feel really good about yourself—and you want to help those around you feel really good about themselves, too. When we see people acting in an abusive, arrogant, or demeaning manner toward others, their behavior almost always is a symptom of their lack of self-esteem. They need to put someone else down to feel good about themselves.

Choose the Right Yardstick

This past year I was diagnosed with cancer and faced the possibility that my life would end sooner than I'd planned. Thankfully, it now looks as if I'll be spared. But the experience has given me important insight into my life.

I have a pretty clear idea of how my ideas have generated enormous revenue for companies that have used my research; I know I've had a substantial impact. But as I've confronted this disease, it's been interesting to see how unimportant that impact is to me now. I've concluded that the metric by which God will assess my life isn't dollars but the individual people whose lives I've touched.

I think that's the way it will work for us all. Don't worry about the level of individual prominence you have achieved; worry about the individuals you have helped become better people. This is my final recommendation: Think about the metric by which your life will be judged, and make a resolution to live every day so that in the end, your life will be judged a success.

CHAPTER 3

Manage Your Work, Manage Your Life

Senior executives have discovered through hard experience that prospering at their level is a matter of carefully combining work and home so as not to lose themselves, their loved ones, or their foothold on success. To learn how they reconcile their professional and personal lives, the authors drew on five years' worth of interviews with almost 4,000 executives worldwide, conducted by students at Harvard Business School, and a survey of 82 executives in an HBS leadership course. The stories and advice of these leaders reflect five main themes: defining success for yourself, managing technology, building support networks at work and at home, traveling or relocating selectively, and collaborating with your partner.

Some intriguing gender differences emerged in the survey data. For example, men still think of their family responsibilities in terms of breadwinning, whereas women often see theirs as role modeling for their children. And male executives tend to praise their partners for making positive contributions to their careers, whereas women praise theirs for not interfering. Executives of both sexes consider the tension between work and family to be primarily a woman's problem, and most of them believe that one can't compete in the global marketplace while leading a "balanced" life. "Earnestly trying to focus," the authors conclude, "is what will see them through."

Work/life balance is at best an elusive ideal and at worst a complete myth, today's senior executives will tell you. But by making deliberate choices about which opportunities they'll pursue and which they'll decline, rather than simply reacting to emergencies, leaders can and do engage meaningfully with work, family, and community. They've discovered through hard experience that prospering in the senior ranks is a matter of carefully combining work and home so as not to lose themselves, their loved ones, or their foothold on success. Those who do this most effectively involve their families in work decisions and activities. They also vigilantly manage their own human capital, endeavoring to give both work and home their due over a period of years, not weeks or days.

That's how the 21st-century business leaders in our research said they reconcile their professional and personal lives. In this article we draw on five years' worth of interviews with almost 4,000 executives worldwide, conducted by students at Harvard Business School, and a survey of 82 executives in an HBS leadership course.

Deliberate choices don't guarantee complete control. Life sometimes takes over, whether it's a parent's dementia or a teenager's car accident. But many of the executives we've studied—men and women alike—have sustained their momentum during such challenges while staying connected to their families. Their stories and advice reflect five main themes: defining success for yourself, managing technology, building support networks at work and at home, traveling or relocating selectively, and collaborating with your partner.

Defining Success for Yourself

When you are leading a major project, you determine early on what a win should look like. The same principle applies to leading a deliberate life: You have to define what success means to you understanding, of course, that your definition will evolve over time.

Executives' definitions of professional and personal success run a gamut from the tactical to the conceptual (see the section "How Leaders Define Work/Life 'Wins'"). For one leader, it means being home at least four nights a week. For another, it means understanding what's going on in the lives of family members. For a third, it's about having emotional energy at both work and home.

How Leaders Define Work/Life "Wins"

In their definitions of professional and personal success, executives highlight these elements:

Some intriguing gender differences emerged in our survey data: In defining professional success, women place more value than men do on individual achievement, having passion for their work, receiving respect, and making a difference, but less value on organizational achievement and ongoing learning and development. A lower percentage of women than of men list financial achievement as an aspect of personal or professional success. Rewarding relationships are by far the most common element of personal success for both sexes, but men list merely having a family as an indicator of success, whereas women describe what a good family life looks like to them. Women are also more likely to mention the importance of friends and community as well as family.

The survey responses consisted of short phrases and lists, but in the interviews executives often defined personal success by telling a story or describing an ideal self or moment in time. Such narratives and self-concepts serve as motivational goalposts, helping people prioritize activities and make sense of conflicts and inconsistencies.

PROFESSIONAL SUCCESS MEANS...

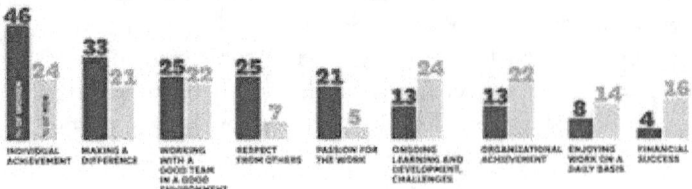

PERSONAL SUCCESS MEANS...

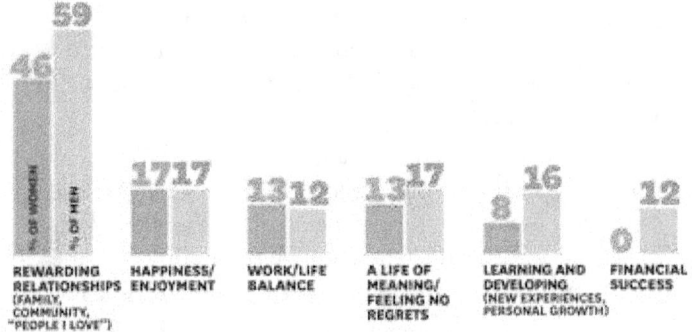

When work and family responsibilities collide, for example, men may lay claim to the cultural narrative of the good provider. Several male executives who admitted to spending inadequate time with their families consider absence an acceptable price for providing their children with opportunities they themselves never had. One of these men, poor during his childhood, said that his financial success both protects his children and validates his parents' struggles. Another even put a positive spin on the breakup of his family: "Looking back, I would have still made a similar decision to focus on work, as I was able to provide for my family and become a leader in my area, and these things were important to me. Now I focus on my kids' education…and spend a lot more time with them over weekends."

Even the men who pride themselves on having achieved some degree of balance between work and other realms of their lives measure themselves against a traditional male ideal. "The 10 minutes I give my kids at night is one million times greater than spending that 10 minutes at work," one interviewee said. It's difficult to imagine a woman congratulating herself for spending 10 minutes a day with her children, but a man may consider the same behavior exemplary.

Indeed, women rarely view themselves as working *for* their families the way men do. Men still think of their family responsibilities in terms of breadwinning, whereas women often see theirs as role modeling for their children. Women emphasize (far more than men do) how important it is for their kids—particularly their daughters—to see them as competent

28

professionals. One said, "I think that work is such a big part of who I am. I want my kids to understand what I do. I am a whole being."

Many women said that the most difficult aspect of managing work and family is contending with cultural expectations about mothering. One admitted that she stopped working at home after her daughter referred to the Bloomberg network as "Mommy's channel." Another commented, "When you are paid well, you can get all the [practical] help you need. What is the most difficult thing, though—what I see my women friends leave their careers for—is the real emotional guilt of not spending enough time with their children. The guilt of *missing out.*"

Both men and women expressed versions of this guilt and associated personal success with not having regrets. They often cope by assigning special significance to a particular metric, such as never missing a Little League game or checking in once a day no matter what. "I just prioritize dinner with my family as if it was a 6 PM meeting with my most important client," said one interviewee. Another offered this suggestion: "Design your house right—have a table in the kitchen where your kids can do homework while your husband cooks and you drink a glass of red wine." Though expressed as advice, this is clearly her very personal, concrete image of what success at home looks like.

Managing Technology

Nearly all the interviewees talked about how critical it is to corral their e-mails, text messages, voice mails, and other communications. Deciding when, where, and how to be accessible for work is an ongoing challenge, particularly for executives with families. Many of them cautioned against using communications technology to be in two places at once, insisting on the value of undivided attention. "When I'm at home, I really am at home," said one. "I force myself to not check my e-mail, take calls, et cetera. I want to give my kids 100% of my attention. But this also works the other way around, because when I'm at work I really want to focus on work. I believe that mixing these spheres too much leads to confusion and mistakes."

That last point is a common concern: Always being plugged in can erode performance. One leader observed that "certain cognitive processes happen when you step away from the frenetic responding to e-mails." (The history of science, after all, is marked by insights that occurred not in the laboratory but while the scientist was engaged in a mundane task—or even asleep.) Another executive pointed out that 24-hour availability can actually hamper initiative in an organization: "If you have weak people who must ask your advice all the time, you feel important. But there is a difference between being truly important and just not letting anyone around you do anything without you."

Strikingly, some people at the top are starting to use communications technology less often while they're working. Several invoked the saying "You can't raise a kid by phone"—and pointed out that it's not the best way to manage a team, either. Often, if it's logistically possible, you're better off communicating in person. How do you know when that's the case? One interviewee made an important distinction between broadcasting information and exchanging and analyzing ideas: "Speaking [on the phone] is easy, but careful, thoughtful listening becomes very challenging. For the most important conversations, I see a real trend moving back to face-to-face. When you're evaluating multibillion-dollar deals…you have to build a bridge to the people."

Deciding when, where, and how to be accessible for work is an ongoing challenge, particularly for executives with families.

When it comes to technology in the home, more than a third of the surveyed executives view it as an invader, and about a quarter see it as a liberator. (The rest are neutral or have mixed feelings.) Some of them resent the smartphone's infringement on family time: "When your phone buzzes," one ruefully noted, it's difficult to "keep your eyes on that soccer field." Others appreciate the flexibility that technology affords them: "I will probably leave here around 4 PM to wrangle my kids," said one participant, "but I will be back and locked into my network and e-mails by 8 PM." Another participant reported, "Sometimes my kids give me a hard time about being on my BlackBerry at the dinner table, but I tell them that my BlackBerry is what enables me to be home with them."

Both camps—those who hate being plugged in and those who love it—acknowledged that executives must learn to manage communications technology wisely. Overall, they view it as a good servant but a bad master. Their advice in this area is quite consistent: Make yourself available but not *too* available to your team; be honest with yourself about how much you can multitask; build relationships and trust through face time; and keep your in-box under control.

Building Support Networks

Across the board, senior executives insisted that managing family and professional life requires a strong network of behind-the-scenes supporters. Absent a primary caregiver who stays at home, they see paid help or assistance from extended family as a necessity. The women in our sample are adamant about this. One said, "We hire people to do the more tactical things—groceries, cooking, helping the children dress—so that we can be there for the most important things." Even interviewees without children said they needed support at home when they became responsible for aging parents or suffered their own health problems.

Emotional support is equally essential. Like anyone else, executives occasionally need to vent when they're dealing with something crazy or irritating at work, and friends and family are a safer audience than colleagues. Sometimes leaders also turn to their personal networks for a fresh perspective on a problem or a decision, because members of their teams don't always have the distance to be objective.

Support at work matters too. Trusted colleagues serve as valuable sounding boards. And many leaders reported that health crises—their own or family members'—might have derailed their careers if not for compassionate bosses and coworkers. The unexpected can waylay even the most carefully planned career.

"When you're young, you think you can control everything," one interviewee said, "but you can't." Executives told stories about heart attacks, cancer, and parents in need of care. One talked about a psychotic reaction to medication. In those situations, mentors and team members helped leaders weather difficult times and eventually return to business as usual.

What about mixing personal and professional networks, since executives must draw on both anyway? That's up for discussion. The men we surveyed tend to prefer separate networks, and the women are pretty evenly split. Interviewees who favor integration said it's a relief to be "the same person" in all contexts and natural to form friendships at work, where they spend most of their time. Those who separate their work lives from their private lives have many reasons for doing so. Some seek novelty and a counterbalance to work. "If all of your socializing centers around your work life, you tend to experience an ever-decreasing circle of influence and ideas," one pointed out. Others want to protect their personal relationships from the churn of the workplace.

Many women keep their networks separate for fear of harming their image. Some never mention their families at work because they don't want to appear unprofessional. A few female executives won't discuss their careers—or even mention that they have jobs—in conversations outside work. But again, not all women reported such conflict between their professional and personal "selves," and several suggested that the tide is turning. One pointed out, "The more women have come into the workplace, the more I talk about my children."

Traveling or Relocating Selectively

Discussions about work/life balance usually focus on managing time. But it's also critical to manage your location—and, more broadly, your role in the global economy. When leaders decide whether to travel or relocate (internationally or domestically), their home lives play a huge part. That's why many of them believe in acquiring global experience and racking up travel miles while they're young and unencumbered. Of those surveyed, 32% said they had turned down an international assignment because they did not want to relocate their families, and 28% said they had done so to protect their marriages.

Many leaders believe in acquiring global experience and racking up travel miles while they're young and unencumbered.Several executives told stories about getting sidetracked or derailed in their careers because a partner or spouse needed to relocate. Of course, travel becomes even trickier with children. Many women reported cutting back on business trips after having children, and several executives of both sexes said they had refused to relocate when their children were adolescents. "When children are very young, they are more mobile," one explained. "But once they are 12 or 13, they want to be in one place."

Female executives are less likely than men to be offered or accept international assignments, in part because of family responsibilities but also because of the restrictive gender roles in certain cultures or perceptions that they are unwilling to relocate. Our survey results—from a well-traveled sample—jibe with student interviewers' qualitative findings. Almost none of the men surveyed (less than 1%, compared with 13% of the women) had turned down an international assignment because of cultural concerns. But for female executives, not all travel is created equal: Gender norms, employment laws, health-care access, and views on work/life balance vary from country to country. One American woman said it requires extra effort in Europe to make sure she doesn't "come off as being intimidating," a concern she attributes in part to being tall. Another woman said that in the Middle East she has had to bring male colleagues to meetings to prove her credibility.

Though women in particular have such difficulties, international assignments are not easy for anyone, and they may simply not be worth it for many executives. Members of both sexes have built gratifying careers while grounding themselves in a particular country or even city. However, if travel is undesirable, ambitious young executives should decide so early on. That way they can avoid getting trapped in an industry that doesn't mesh with their geographic preferences and give themselves time to find ways other than travel to signal open-mindedness, sophistication, skill diversity, and willingness to go above and beyond. (Several executives noted that international experience is often viewed as a sign of those personal attributes.) "International experience can be helpful," one executive observed, "but it's just as important to have had exposure across the business lines. Both allow you to understand that not everybody thinks as you do." Some executives even question the future of globe-hopping, noting that carbon costs, fuel costs, and security concerns may tighten future travel budgets.

Collaborating with Your Partner

Managing yourself, technology, networks, travel—it's a tall order. Leaders with strong family lives spoke again and again of needing a shared vision of success for everyone at home—not just for themselves. Most of the executives in our sample have partners or spouses, and common goals hold those couples together. Their relationships offer both partners opportunities—for uninterrupted (or less interrupted) work, for adventurous travel, for intensive parenting, for political or community impact—that they might not otherwise have had.

About the Research

Since 2008 more than 600 students in Harvard Business School's second-year Managing Human Capital course have interviewed 3,850 C-suite executives and leaders (of whom 655 were CEOs, presidents, or board members) at companies and nonprofits around the world.

The goal? To gain greater insight into how today's top leaders make choices in their professional and personal lives. This project has been a true partnership between the students and the executives. Everyone involved wanted to deeply explore what it means for leaders to manage their human capital in the 21st century and more specifically, in the wake of the recent global recession.

The executives were a diverse group (44% female, 56% male) and represented a wide range of industries, including finance, retail, energy, health care, and technology. They came from 51 countries, and 45% of them had worked in countries other than the United States.

The interviews were semistructured: As long as students related their questions to topics covered in Managing Human Capital, they were allowed considerable leeway in what to ask and how far to go in following up on responses. That way they could dig into the issues they found most compelling.

To supplement the interviews, we surveyed 82 senior executives who were attending a 2012 leadership course at HBS. We asked them about their experiences managing their careers and families. The sample consisted of 58 men and 24 women from 33 countries in Africa, Europe, Asia, the Middle East, and North and South America. Statistics in the article come from the survey data, and quotations come from the field data.

Leaders also emphasized the importance of complementary relationships. Many said how much they value their partners' emotional intelligence, task focus, big-picture thinking, detail orientation—in short, whatever cognitive or behavioral skills balance out their own tendencies. And many of those we surveyed consider emotional support the biggest contribution their partners have made to their careers. Both men and women often mentioned that their partners believe in them or have urged them to take business risks or pursue job opportunities that were not immediately rewarding but led to longer-term satisfaction. They also look to their partners to be sounding boards and honest critics. One executive said that her partner asks "probing questions to challenge my thinking so I can be better prepared for an opposing viewpoint."

What Partners Contribute

Executives say that their partners and spouses share their vision of success, bring complementary skills, and provide the following types of support:

A partner's support may come in many forms, but what it almost always boils down to is making sure the executive manages his or her own human capital effectively. The pressures and demands on executives are intense, multidirectional, and unceasing. Partners can help them keep their eyes on what matters, budget their time and energy, live healthfully, and make deliberate choices—sometimes tough ones—about work, travel, household management, and community involvement.

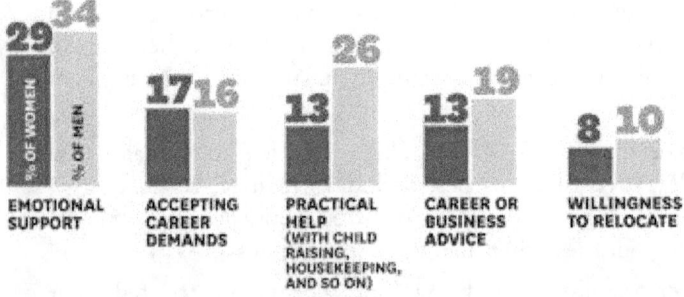

Men, however, appear to be getting more spousal support overall. Male interviewees—many of whom have stay-at-home wives—often spoke of their spouses' willingness to take care of children, tolerate long work hours, and even relocate, sometimes as a way of life. But by and large, they no longer seem to expect the classic 1950s "corporate wife," who hosted dinners for the boss and cocktail parties for clients. (Exceptions exist in some countries and industries. One male executive who works in oil fields said, "When you are living and working in those camp environments, it is indispensable to have your wife talk with other spouses.") Men frequently noted that their partners won't allow them to neglect their families, health, or social lives. For example: "My wife is militant about family dinner, and I am home every night for dinner even if I have to work afterward."

Women, by contrast, slightly more often mentioned their partners' willingness to free them from traditional roles at home. One explained, in a typical comment, "He understands the demands of my role and does not put pressure on me when work takes more time than I would like." In other words, male executives tend to praise their partners for making positive contributions to their careers, whereas women praise theirs for not interfering.

When we look at the survey data, we see other striking differences between the sexes. Fully 88% of the men are married, compared with 70% of the women. And 60% of the men have spouses who don't work full-time outside the home, compared with only 10% of the women. The men have an average of 2.22 children; the women, 1.67.

What Tomorrow's Leaders Think

The fact that the interviewees all agreed to take time from their hectic schedules to share their insights with students might introduce a selection effect. Busy leaders who choose to help students presumably value interpersonal relationships. Because they're inclined to reflect on work and life, they're probably also making deliberate choices in both realms—and they certainly have enough money to pay for support at home. All that may explain why many interviewees reported being basically happy despite their struggles and why few mentioned serious damage to their marriages or families due to career pressures. This sample is an elite group of people better positioned than most to achieve work/life balance. That they nevertheless consider it an impossible task suggests a sobering reality for the rest of us.

Our student interviewers say, almost universally, that the leaders they spoke with dispensed valuable advice about how to maintain both a career and a family. One interviewer reported, "All acknowledged making sacrifices and concessions at times but emphasized the important role that supportive spouses and families played." Still, many students are alarmed at how much leaders sacrifice at home and how little headway the business world has made in adapting to families' needs.

Executives of both sexes consider the tension between work and family to be primarily a women's problem.

Male executives admitted that they don't prioritize their families enough. And women are more likely than men to have forgone kids or marriage to avoid the pressures of combining work and family. One said, "Because I'm not a mother, I haven't experienced the major driver of inequality: having children." She added, "People assume that if you don't have kids, then you either can't have kids or else you're a hard-driving bitch. So I haven't had any negative career repercussions, but I've probably been judged personally."

Executives of both sexes consider the tension between work and family to be primarily a women's problem, and the students find that discouraging. "Given that leadership positions in corporations around the world are still dominated by men," one explained, "I fear that it will take many organizations much longer than it should to make accommodations for women to…effectively manage their careers and personal lives."

Students also resist leaders' commonly held belief that you can't compete in the global marketplace while leading a "balanced" life. When one executive argued that it's impossible to have "a great family life, hobbies, and an amazing career" all at the same time, the student interviewing him initially thought, "That's his perspective." But after more conversations with leaders? "Every single executive confirmed this view in one way or another, and I came to believe that it is the reality of today's business world." It remains to be seen whether, and how, that reality can be changed for tomorrow.We can't predict what the workplace or the family will look like later in this century, or how the two institutions will coexist. But we can assert three simple truths:

Life happens.

Even the most dedicated executive may suddenly have his or her priorities upended by a personal crisis—a heart attack, for instance, or a death in the family. As one pointed out, people tend to ignore work/life balance until "something is wrong." But that kind of disregard is a choice, and not a wise one. Since when do smart executives assume that everything will work out just fine? If that approach makes no sense in the boardroom or on the factory floor, it makes no sense in one's personal life.

There are multiple routes to success.

Some people plan their careers in detail; others grab whatever opportunity presents itself. Some stick with one company, building political capital and a deep knowledge of the organization's culture and resources; others change employers frequently, relying on external contacts and a fresh perspective to achieve success. Similarly, at home different solutions work for different individuals and families. Some executives have a stay-at-home partner; others make trade-offs to enable both partners to work. The questions of child care, international postings, and smartphones at the dinner table don't have "right" answers. But the questions need to be asked.

No one can do it alone.

Of the many paths to success, none can be walked alone. A support network is crucial both at and outside work—and members of that network must get their needs met too. In pursuit of rich professional and personal lives, men and women will surely continue to face tough decisions about where to concentrate their efforts. Our research suggests that earnestly trying to focus is what will see them through.

CHAPTER 4

Balance Your Life

Skills for integrating every part of your life, by Stewart D. Friedman

OVERCOMMITTED. DISTRACTED. STRESSED OUT. STRETCHED TOO THIN. This is how many of us describe ourselves today. I hear it from men and women; from the young and the old; from executives, MBA students, doctors, retailers, artisans, research scientists, soldiers, stay-at-home parents, teachers, and engineers around the world. In an age of constant communication and economic pressure, everyone is struggling to have meaningful work, domestic bliss, community engagement, and a satisfying inner life. Some have already given up on the idea of having it all: As I discovered last year in a study comparing undergraduates from the classes of 1992 and 2012 at the University of Pennsylvania's Wharton School, a significant number of Millennials (the generation born from 1980 to 2000) are deciding not to become parents, because they don't see how they can fit children into their busy lives.

A commitment to better "work/life balance" isn't the solution. As I've argued for a long time and as many more people are now asserting balance is bunk. It's a misguided metaphor because it assumes we must always make trade-offs among the four main aspects of our lives: work or school, home or family (however you define that), community (friends, neighbors, religious or social groups), and self (mind, body, spirit). A more realistic and more gratifying goal is better integration between work and the rest of life through the pursuit of *four-way wins,* which improve performance in all four dimensions.

Such integration starts with embracing three key principles be real, be whole, and be innovative. It takes certain skills to bring those principles to life. In my 30 years as a professor, researcher, consultant, and executive, as I've studied and served thousands of people, I've found 18 specific skills that foster greater alignment and harmony among the four life domains. In this article I describe those skills and offer exercises drawn from the latest findings in organizational psychology and related fields to help you hone a few of the skills that business professionals often find most difficult to master. While there's more you can do to instill the three principles, the advice offered here will help you move down the right path.

Skills for Being Real

For well over a decade I've run a program called Total Leadership that teaches the three principles to executives, MBA candidates, and many others. It starts with a focus on being real how to act with authenticity by clarifying what's important, wherever you are, whatever you're doing.

That requires you to:

1. Know what matters.
2. Embody values consistently.
3. Align actions with values.
4. Convey values with stories.
5. Envision your legacy.
6. Hold yourself accountable.

The ability to do the first two things is especially crucial. Let's begin with how to know what matters. One exercise that enhances this skill, called *four circles,* has you examine the importance and congruence of your various roles and responsibilities in life. (You can do it online at this free site: www.myfourcircles.com.) You start by drawing circles representing the four domains work, home, community, and self varying the sizes to reflect how much you value each. Next you move the circles to show whether and to what degree they overlap. At this point you think about the values, goals, interests, actions, and results you pursue in each domain. Are they compatible or in opposition? Imagine what your life would be like if your aspirations in all four circles, and the means by which you achieved them, lined up perfectly, like the concentric rings of a tree trunk. For most of us that's an unattainable ideal, but what actions could you realistically take to move toward that kind of overlap? Could you change how you work, or even how you think about the purpose of your work, without diminishing the personal value you derive from it? Could you help your family to better see how your business life benefits them so that they would be more supportive of it?

A complementary exercise, called *conversation starter,* encourages people to embody values consistently. This involves bringing an object from your nonwork life (such as a family photograph, a travel memento, or a trophy) into the office. If a colleague mentions it, you explain what this part of your life means to you *and* how it helps you at work. Then you consider asking that person to bring his or her own conversation starter. You might also take something from your work to your home and talk to your roommates, spouse, kids, or dinner guests about it. Tell them about what you do and who you are in your role at work, focusing especially on what this might mean for them.

When Victoria, the head of marketing for a pharmaceutical company division, drew her four circles, she initially placed the biggest one, representing work, apart from all the rest. She didn't see any real connection between her professional identity and her home, community, and inner lives. But when she began to talk about the separation with a few colleagues, friends, and family members, she came to realize that one major aspect of her mission as an executive promoting greater health was a lot more compatible with her other circles than she had thought.

She could also see how just a few small changes in approach might create much more overlap. For example, at home she started to talk more with her two daughters about the social impact of her business, sharing stories about all the ways in which her company's medicines were saving lives. The girls responded with greater pride in, and understanding of, their mom's commitment to work. As a team leader, Victoria began to reframe core drug-marketing tasks in terms of the products' benefits to end users who were all the children, spouses, parents, siblings, friends, or neighbors of someone just like the families and communities she and her employees had. As a result, her group became more impassioned and hardworking, which ultimately eased her load and gave her more time for other pursuits. Perhaps most important, Victoria felt less guilt about the way she was spending her time and energy, and newly secure in her mission at the office as well as in her family's support.

Skills for Being Whole

The second principle that Total Leadership addresses is being whole or acting with integrity. What I mean by that is respecting the fact that all the roles you play make up one whole person and encouraging others to view you the same way. To do that you must be able to:

1. Clarify expectations.
2. Help others.
3. Build supportive networks.
4. Apply all your resources.
5. Manage boundaries intelligently.
6. Weave disparate strands.

One of the most important skills here is knowing how to apply all your resources (such as your knowledge, skills, and contacts) in the various domains of your life to benefit the other domains. An exercise that helps you do that is called *talent transfer*. It involves writing a résumé listing all the skills you've developed from mentoring colleagues, organizing family activities, or running a church bake sale and thinking of how each might be used to achieve different ends. Organizational psychologists call this a strength development approach: You identify your talents and then apply them in new areas, enhancing them further. Another way to do this is to reflect on something that makes you feel good a work accomplishment, a fruitful friendship, your commitment to salsa dancing and then consider an area of your life you'd like to improve. How might the skills you used to achieve the former help you in the latter?

To manage boundaries intelligently is another key challenge. I advise people to practice something I call *segment and merge,* and then decide which strategy works best when. First, think about ways to create separation (in time and space) between your different roles. You might try setting limits on yourself. For example, if there's an ambitious work project that you've been putting off, try dedicating the first two hours of each Saturday morning for the next month to tackling it, and then give yourself the rest of the day off. Or, if your job keeps monopolizing your evenings, you might experiment with a "no smartphones at the dinner table" policy. Now do the opposite: Think about opportunities to bring together two or more parts of your life. You might take a child to a company-sponsored charity run or bring a coworker to a block party in your neighborhood. After you've tried a new way of segmenting and a new way of merging, jot down your insights about what worked and what didn't, for both you and the people around you. Were you more or less productive? Did you find yourself more or less distracted? How did others react? Were they put off, or did they seem to feel closer to and more trusting of you?

An example of the segmenting concept in action comes from Brian, a manager in an accounting firm. In a monthlong experiment, he set aside his 40-minute train rides to and from work solely for "downtime." He caught up on e-mails to family and friends and invested in his own development through reading and reflection for example, by diagramming the factors affecting his sense of stability, including his stress and energy levels and his feelings about himself, his relationships, and his future. Sometimes, as an alternative to that inward focus, he had conversations with the neighbors, colleagues, and acquaintances he sat next to on the train, exchanging advice about everything from child care to real estate. This simple reallocation of commuting time from doing work to other things resulted, perhaps paradoxically, in Brian's being better prepared for work and more proactive about his career progression. He also felt closer to his extended family and the old friends with whom he'd reconnected and to the people in his local community, because he was engaging with more of them on his way to the office and back. Having an after-work buffer period allowed him to reenter his home with less stress and more openness and to develop new insights about how he could be a better father and husband. Personally, he also felt "more grounded and less crazed." He came to see more clearly the positive impact of rest and recovery on his performance, which led him to experiment with increasing his sleep time by about an hour a day. Again, the small shift in boundaries significantly boosted his productivity, well-being, and relationships. Everyone with whom he interacted daily noticed that he was less cranky and more energetic.

Skills for Being Innovative

The third Total Leadership principle is to be innovative to act with creativity in identifying and pursuing more four-way wins. To do so, you need to:

1. Focus on results.
2. Resolve conflicts among domains.
3. Challenge the status quo.
4. See new ways of doing things.
5. Embrace change courageously.
6. Create cultures of innovation around you.

Scenario exercises are one of several effective methods of increasing your capacity to focus on results, especially on the quality of your contributions rather than the amount of time or energy you spend on them. Scenarios involve identifying a specific goal you want to achieve and then listing three alternative ways to get there, including the resources you'll need and the challenges you'll face. This sort of brainstorming encourages you to keep your eyes on the prize. Another method is experimenting with new patterns of behavior, trying activities at new times or in different places. It could be something as simple as shaving at the gym instead of at home, or practicing your trumpet at the office after hours rather than disturbing your neighbors at home. What were the pros and cons of switching up your routine?

How did it affect your results?

Crowdsourcing is an exercise that helps you practice how to see new ways of doing things. To try this, gather a group of your most creative friends and describe a problem you're facing. Then ask for ideas about potential solutions and record what you hear. Select the one you think wisest, draft a plan, and try to make it happen. Stay in touch with your advisers, at least weekly, and after a month or so review your results with them. If the approach you tried didn't work, or if you need more time to solve the problem, tweak your behavior or try another idea altogether, drawing on what you learned from the first experiment.

Former Bain & Company CEO Tom Tierney took not months but years to think about and solicit advice on what would eventually become the Bridgespan Group -- an independent nonprofit that was incubated in and then spun out of Bain—which provides strategic consulting and leadership development to philanthropists, foundations, and other nonprofit organizations. In the 1980s he began to think, write, and talk about his idea for what he then generically called "Make a Difference Company," picking the brains of colleagues and friends, including the likes of the presidential adviser and founder of Common Cause, John Gardner. Emboldened by those conversations, Tierney at first took small steps to move closer to his vision by, for example, volunteering for the United Way of the Bay Area while he was running Bain's San Francisco office and eventually joining the nonprofit's board. This was the first of many on which he would serve. In 1999, Tierney folded all that experience, knowledge, and crowdsourced wisdom into Bridgespan, and a year later he stepped down as chief executive of Bain to focus on the new organization.

The Idea in Brief

Skills for integrating every part of your life. Three principles, the advice offered here will help you move down the right path.

Skills for Being Real

Total leadership starts with a focus on being real how to act with authenticity by clarifying what's important, wherever you are, whatever you're doing.

That requires you to:

1. Know what matters.
2. Embody values consistently.
3. Align actions with values.
4. Convey values with stories.
5. Envision your legacy.
6. Hold yourself accountable.

Skills for Being Whole

The second principle that Total Leadership addresses is being whole or acting with integrity. That is respecting the fact that all the roles you play make up one whole person and encouraging others to view you the same way. To do that you must be able to:

1. Clarify expectations.
2. Help others.
3. Build supportive networks.
4. Apply all your resources.
5. Manage boundaries intelligently.
6. Weave disparate strands.

Skills for Being Innovative

The third Total Leadership principle is to be innovative to act with creativity in identifying and pursuing more four-way wins. To do so, you need to:

1. Focus on results.
2. Resolve conflicts among domains.
3. Challenge the status quo.
4. See new ways of doing things.
5. Embrace change courageously.
6. Create cultures of innovation around you.

CHAPTER 5

Have a Richer Life

Traditional thinking pits work and the rest of our lives against each other. But taking smart steps to integrate work, home, community, and self will make you a more productive leader and a more fulfilled person. by Stewart D. Friedman

In my research and coaching work over the past two decades, I have met many people who feel unfulfilled, overwhelmed, or stagnant because they are forsaking performance in one or more aspects of their lives. They aren't bringing their leadership abilities to bear in all of life's domains work, home, community, and self (mind, body, and spirit). Of course, there will always be some tension among the different roles we play. But, contrary to the common wisdom, there's no reason to assume that it's a zero-sum game. It makes more sense to pursue excellent performance as a leader in all four domains—achieving what I call "four-way wins" not trading off one for another but finding mutual value among them. This is the main idea in a program called Total Leadership that I teach at the Wharton School and at companies and workshops around the world. "Total" because it's about the whole person and "Leadership" because it's about creating sustainable change to benefit not just you but the most important people around you.

Scoring four-way wins starts by taking a clear view of what you want from and can contribute to each domain of your life, now and in the future, with thoughtful consideration of the people who matter most to you and the expectations you have for one another. This is followed by systematically designing and implementing carefully crafted experiments—doing something new for a short period to see how it affects all four domains. If an experiment doesn't work out, you stop or adjust, and little is lost. If it does work out, it's a small win; over time these add up so that your overall efforts are focused increasingly on what and who matter most. Either way, you learn more about how to lead in all parts of your life.

This process doesn't require inordinate risk. On the contrary, it works because it entails realistic expectations, short-term changes that are in your control, and the explicit support of those around you. Take, for instance, Kenneth Chen, a manager I met at a workshop in 2005. (All names in this article are pseudonyms.) His professional goal was to become CEO, but he had other goals as well, which on the face of it might have appeared conflicting. He had recently moved to Philadelphia and wanted to get more involved with his community. He also wished to strengthen bonds with his family. To further all of these goals, he decided to join a citybased community board, which would not only allow him to hone his leadership skills (in support of his professional goal) but also have benefits in the family domain. It would give him more in common with his sister, a teacher who gave back to the community every day, and he hoped his fiancée would participate as well, enabling them to do something together for the greater good. He would feel more spiritually alive and this, in turn, would increase his self-confidence at work.

Now, about three years later, he reports that he is not only on a community board with his fiancée but also on the formal succession track for CEO. He's a better leader in all aspects of his life because he is acting in ways that are more consistent with his values. He is creatively enhancing his performance in all domains of his life and leading others to improve their performance by encouraging them to better integrate the different parts of their lives, too.

Kenneth is not alone. Workshop participants assess themselves at the beginning and the end of the program, and they consistently report improvements in their effectiveness, as well as a greater sense of harmony among the once-competing domains of their lives. In a study over a four-month period of more than 300 business professionals (whose average age was about 35), their *satisfaction* increased by an average of 20% in their work lives, 28% in their home lives, and 31% in their community lives. Perhaps most significant, their satisfaction in the domain of the self their physical and emotional health and their intellectual and spiritual growth increased by 39%. But they also reported that their *performance* improved: at work (by 9%), at home (15%), in the community (12%), and personally (25%). Paradoxically, these gains were made even as participants spent less time on work and more on other aspects of their lives. They're working smarter and they're more focused, passionate, and committed to what they're doing.

While hundreds of leaders at all levels go through this program every year, you don't need a workshop to identify worthwhile experiments. The process is pretty straightforward, though not simple. In the sections that follow, I will give you an overview of the process and take you through the basics of designing and implementing experiments to produce four-way wins.

The Total Leadership Process

The Total Leadership concept rests on three principles:

1. Be real: Act with authenticity by clarifying what's important.
2. Be whole: Act with integrity by respecting the whole person.
3. Be innovative: Act with creativity by experimenting with how things get done.

You begin the process by thinking, writing, and talking with peer coaches to identify your core values, your leadership vision, and the current alignment of your actions and values clarifying what's important. Peer coaching is enormously valuable, at this stage and throughout, because an outside perspective provides a sounding board for your ideas, challenges you, gives you a fresh way to see the possibilities for innovation, and helps hold you accountable to your commitments.

You then identify the most important people—"key stakeholders"—in all domains and the performance expectations you have of one another. Then you talk with them: If you're like most participants, you'll be surprised to find that what, and how much, your key stakeholders actually need from you is different from, and less than, what you thought beforehand.

These insights create opportunities for you to focus your attention more intelligently, spurring innovative action. Now, with a firmer grounding in what's most important, and a more complete picture of your inner circle, you begin to see new ways of making life better, not just for you but for the people around you. The next step is to design experiments and then try them out during a controlled period of time. The best experiments are changes that your stakeholders wish for as much as, if not more than, you do.

Designing Experiments.

To pursue a four-way win means to produce a change intended to fulfill multiple goals that benefit each and every domain of your life. In the domain of work, typical goals for an experiment can be captured under these broad headings: taking advantage of new opportunities for increasing productivity, reducing hidden costs, and improving the work environment. Goals for home and community tend to revolve around improving relationships and contributing more to society.

For the self, it's usually about improving health and finding greater meaning in life. As you think through the goals for your experiment, keep in mind the interests and opinions of your key stakeholders and anyone else who might be affected by the changes you are envisioning. In exploring the idea of joining a community board, for instance, Kenneth Chen sought advice from his boss, who had served on many boards, and also from the company's charitable director and the vice president of talent. In this way, he got their support. His employers could see how his participation on a board would benefit the company by developing Kenneth's leadership skills and his social network.

Some experiments benefit only a single domain directly while having indirect benefits in the others. For example, setting aside three mornings a week to exercise improves your health directly but may indirectly give you more energy for your work and raise your self-esteem, which in turn might make you a better father and friend. Other activities such as running a half-marathon with your kids to raise funds for a charity sponsored by your company occur in, and directly benefit, all four domains simultaneously. Whether the benefits are direct or indirect, achieving a four-way win is the goal. That's what makes the changes sustainable: Everyone benefits. The expected gains need not accrue until sometime in the future, so keep in mind that some benefits may not be obvious far-off career advancements, for instance, or a contact who might ultimately offer valuable connections.

Identify possibilities.

Open your mind to what's possible and try to think of as many potential experiments as you can, describing in a sentence or two what you would do in each. This is a time to let your imagination run free. Don't worry about all the potential obstacles at this point.

At first blush, conceiving of experiments that produce benefits for all the different realms may seem a formidable task. After all, if it were easy, people wouldn't be feeling so much tension between work and the rest of their lives. But I've found that most people realize it's not that hard once they approach the challenge systematically. And, like a puzzle, it can be fun, especially if you keep in mind that experiments must fit your particular circumstances.

Experiments can and do take myriad forms. But having sifted through hundreds of experiment designs, my research team and I have found that they tend to fall into nine general types. Use the nine categories described in the section "How Can I Design an Experiment to Improve All Domains of My Life?" to organize your thinking.

One category of experiment involves changes in where and when work gets done. One workshop participant, a sales director for a global cement producer, tried working online from his local public library one day a week to free himself from his very long commute. This was a break from a company culture that didn't traditionally support employees working remotely, but the change benefited everyone. He had more time for outside interests, and he was more engaged and productive at work.

Another category has to do with regular self-reflection. As an example, you might keep a record of your activities, thoughts, and feelings over the course of a month to see how various actions influence your performance and quality of life. Still another category focuses on planning and organizing your time—such as trying out a new technology that coordinates commitments at work with those in the other domains.

Conversations about work and the rest of life tend to emphasize segmentation: How do I shut out the office when I am with my family? How can I eliminate distractions and concentrate purely on work? But, in some cases, it might be better to make boundaries between domains more permeable, not thicker. The very technologies that make it hard for us to maintain healthy boundaries among domains also enable us to blend them in ways unfathomable even a decade ago that can render us more productive and more fulfilled. These tools give us choices. The challenge we all face is learning how to use them wisely, and smart experiments give you an opportunity to increase your skill in doing so. The main point is to identify possibilities that will work well in your unique situation.

All effective experiments require that you question traditional assumptions about how things get done, as the sales director did. It's easier to feel free to do this, and to take innovative action, when you know that your goal is to improve performance in all domains and that you'll be gathering data about the impact of your experiment to determine if indeed it is working for your key stakeholders and for you.

Whatever type you choose, the most useful experiments feel like something of a stretch: not too easy, not too daunting. It might be something quite mundane for someone else, but that doesn't matter. What's critical is that *you* see it as a moderately difficult challenge.

Choose a few, get started, and adapt.

Coming up with possibilities is an exercise in unbounded imagination. But when it comes time to take action, it's not practical to try out more than three experiments at once. Typically, two turn out to be relatively successful and one goes haywire, so you will earn some small wins, and learn something useful about leadership, without biting off more than you can chew. Now the priority is to narrow the list to the three most-promising candidates by reviewing which will:

- Give you the best overall return on your investment

- Be the most costly in regret and missed opportunities if you don't do it

- Allow you to practice the leadership skills you most want to develop

- Be the most fun by involving more of what you want to be doing

- Move you furthest toward your vision of how you want to lead your life

Once you choose and begin to move down the road with your experiment, however, be prepared to adapt to the unforeseen. Don't become too wedded to the details of any one experiment's plan, because you will at some point be surprised and need to adjust. An executive I'll call Lim, for example, chose as one experiment to run the Chicago Marathon. He had been feeling out of shape, which in turn diminished his energy and focus both at work and at home. His wife, Joanne, was pregnant with their first child and initially supported the plan because she believed that the focus required by the training and the physical outlet it provided would make Lim a better father. The family also had a strong tradition of athleticism, and Joanne herself was an accomplished athlete. Lim was training with his boss and other colleagues, and all agreed that it would be a healthy endeavor that would improve professional communication (as they thought there would be plenty of time to bond during training).

But as her delivery date approached, Joanne became apprehensive, which she expressed to Lim as concern that he might get injured. Her real concern, though, was that he was spending so much time on an activity that might drain his energy at a point when the family needed him most. One adjustment that Lim made to reassure Joanne of his commitment to their family was to initiate another experiment in which he took the steps needed to allow him to work at home on Thursday afternoons. He had to set up some new technologies and agree to send a monthly memo to his boss summarizing what he was accomplishing on those afternoons. He also bought a baby sling, which would allow him to keep his new son with him while at home. In the end, not only were Joanne and their baby on hand to cheer Lim on while he ran the marathon, but she ended up joining him for the second half of the race to give him a boost when she saw his energy flagging. His business unit's numbers improved during the period when he was training and working at home. So did the unit's morale people began to see the company as more flexible, and they were encouraged to be more creative in how they got their own work done and word got around. Executives throughout the firm began to come up with their own ideas for ways to pay more attention to other sides of their employees' lives and so build a stronger sense of community at work.

The investment in a well-designed experiment almost always pays off because you learn how to lead in new and creative ways in all parts of your life. And if your experiments turn out well as they usually, but not always, do it will benefit everyone: you, your business, your family, and your community.

Measuring Progress

The only way to fail with an experiment is to fail to learn from it, and this makes useful metrics essential. No doubt it's better to achieve the results you are after than to fall short, but hitting targets does not in itself advance you toward becoming the leader you want to be. Failed experiments give you, and those around you, information that helps create better ones in the future.

The exhibit "How Do I Know If My Experiment Is Working?" shows how Kenneth Chen measured his progress. He used this simple chart to spell out the intended benefits of his experiment in each of the four domains and how he would assess whether he had realized these benefits. To set up your own scorecard, use a separate sheet for each experiment; at the top of the page, write a brief description of it. Then record your goals for each domain in the first column. In the middle column, describe your results metrics: how you will measure whether the goals for each domain have been achieved. In the third column, describe your action metrics the plan for the steps you will take to implement your experiment. As you begin to implement your plan, you may find that your initial indicators are too broad or too vague, so refine your scorecard as you go along to make it more useful for you. The main point is to have practical ways of measuring your outcomes and your progress toward them, and the approach you take only needs to work for you and your stakeholders.

Workshop participants have used all kinds of metrics: cost savings from reduced travel, number of e-mail misunderstandings averted, degree of satisfaction with family time, hours spent volunteering at a teen center, and so on. Metrics may be objective or subjective, qualitative or quantitative, reported by you or by others, and frequently or intermittently observed. When it comes to frequency, for instance, it helps to consider how long you'll be able to remember what you did. For example, if you were to go on a diet to get healthier, increase energy, and enhance key relationships, food intake would be an important metric. But would you be able to remember what you ate two days ago?

Small Wins for Big Change

Experiments shouldn't be massive, allencompassing shifts in the way you live. Highly ambitious designs usually fail because they're too much to handle. The best experiments let you try something new while minimizing the inevitable risks associated with change. When the stakes are smaller, it's easier to overcome the fear of failure that inhibits innovation. You start to see results, and others take note, which both inspires you to go further and builds support from your key stakeholders.

Another benefit of the small-wins approach to experiments is that it opens doors that would otherwise be closed. You can say to people invested in the decision, "Let's just try this. If it doesn't work, we'll go back to the old way or try something different." By framing an experiment as a trial, you reduce resistance because people are more likely to try something new if they know it's not permanent and if they have control over deciding whether the experiment is working according to *their* performance expectations.

But "small" is a relative term what might look like a small step for you could seem like a giant leap to me, and vice versa. So don't get hung up on the word. What's more, this isn't about the scope or importance of the changes you eventually make. Large-scale change is grounded in small steps toward a big idea. So while the steps in an experiment might be small, the goals are not. Ismail, a successful 50-year-old entrepreneur and CEO of an engineering services company, described the goal for his first experiment this way: "Restructure my company and my role in it." There's nothing small about that. He felt he was missing a sense of purpose.

Ismail designed practical steps that would allow him to move toward his large goal over time. His first experiments were small and achievable. He introduced a new method that both his colleagues and his wife could use to communicate with him. He began to hold sacrosanct time for his family and his church. As he looked for ways to free up more time, he initiated delegation experiments that had the effect of flattening his organization's structure. These small wins crossed over several domains, and eventually he did indeed transform his company and his own role in it. When I spoke with him 18 months after he'd started, he acknowledged that he'd had a hard time coping with the loss of control over tactical business matters, but he described his experiments as "a testament to the idea of winning the small battles and letting the war be won as a result." He and his leadership team both felt more confident about the firm's new organizational structure.

How Can I Design an Experiment to Improve All Domains of My Life?

Our research has revealed that most successful experiments combine components of nine general categories. Thinking about possibilities in this way will make it easier for you to conceive of the small changes you can make that will mutually benefit your work, your home, your community, and yourself. Most experiments are a hybrid of some combination of these categories.

Tracking and Reflecting

Keeping a record of activities, thoughts, and feelings (and perhaps distributing it to friends, family, and coworkers) to assess progress on personal and professional goals, thereby increasing self-awareness and maintaining priorities. **Examples:**

- Record visits to the gym along with changes in energy levels
- Track the times of day when you feel most engaged or most lethargic

Planning and Organizing

Taking actions designed to better use time and prepare and plan for the future. **Examples:**

- Use a PDA for all activities, not just work
- Share your schedule with someone else
- Prepare for the week on Sunday evening

Rejuvenating and Restoring

Attending to body, mind, and spirit so that the tasks of daily living and working are undertaken with renewed power, focus, and commitment. **Examples:**

- Quit unhealthy physical habits (smoking, drinking)
- Make time for reading a novel
- Engage in activities that improve emotional and spiritual health (yoga, meditation, etc.)

Appreciating and Caring

Having fun with people (typically, by doing things with coworkers outside work), caring for others, and appreciating relationships as a way of bonding at a basic human level to respect the whole person, which increases trust. **Examples:**

- Join a book group or health club with coworkers
- Help your son complete his homework
- Devote one day a month to community service

Focusing and Concentrating

Being physically present, psychologically present, or both when needed to pay attention to stakeholders who matter most. Sometimes this means saying no to opportunities or obligations. Includes attempts to show more respect to important people encountered in different domains and the need to be accessible to them. **Examples:**

- Turn off digital communication devices at a set time
- Set aside a specific time to focus on one thing or person
- Review e-mail at preset times during the day

Revealing and Engaging

Sharing more of yourself with others—and listening—so they can better support your values and the steps you want to take toward your leadership vision. By enhancing communication about different aspects of life, you demonstrate respect for the whole person. **Examples:**

- Have weekly conversations about religion with spouse
- Describe your vision to others
- Mentor a new employee

Time Shifting and "Re-Placing"

Working remotely or during different hours to increase flexibility and thus better fit in community, family, and personal activities while increasing efficiency; questioning traditional assumptions and trying new ways to get things done. **Examples:**

- Work from home
- Take music lessons during your lunch hour
- Do work during your commute

Delegating and Developing

Reallocating tasks in ways that increase trust, free up time, and develop skills in yourself and others; working smarter by reducing or eliminating low-priority activities. **Examples:**

- Hire a personal assistant
- Have a subordinate take on some of your responsibilities

Exploring and Venturing

Taking steps toward a new job, career, or other activity that better aligns your work, home, community, and self with your core values and aspirations. **Examples:**

- Take on new roles at work, such as a cross-functional assignment
- Try a new coaching style
- Join the board of your child's day care center

How Do I Know If My Experiment Is Working?

Using this tool, an executive I'll call Kenneth Chen systematically set out in detail his various goals, the metrics he would use to measure his progress, and the steps he would take in conducting an experiment that would further those goals joining the board of a nonprofit organization. Kenneth's work sheet is merely an example: Every person's experiments, goals, and metrics are unique.

EXPERIMENT'S GOALS HOW I WILL MEASURE SUCCESS IMPLEMENTATION STEPS

Work

To fulfill the expectation that executives will give back to the local community To establish networks with other officers in my

company and other professionals in the area To learn leadership skills from other board members and from the organization I join Collect business cards from everyone I meet on the board and during board meetings, and keep track of the number of professionals I meet After each meeting, regularly record the leadership skills of those I would like to emulate Meet with my manager, who has sat on many boards and can provide support and advice

- Meet with the director of my company's foundation to determine my real interests and to help assess what relationship
- our firm has with various community organizations
- Discuss my course of action with my fiancée and see whether joining a board interests her
- Sign up to attend the December 15 overview session of the Business on Board program
- Assess different opportunities within the community and then reach out to organizations I'm interested in
- Apply for membership to a community board

Home

To join a board that can involve my fiancée, Celine To have something to discuss with my sister (a special-education instructor)

See whether Celine gets involved in the board Record the number of conversations my sister and I have about community service for the next three months and see whether they have brought us closer

Community

- To provide my leadership skills to a nonprofit organization
- To get more involved in giving back to the community
- Record what I learn about each nonprofit organization I research
- Record the number of times I attend board meetings

Self

- To feel good about contributing to others' welfare
- To see others grow as a result of my efforts
- To become more compassionate
- Assess how I feel about myself in a daily journal
- Assess the effect I have on others in terms of potential number of people affected Ask for feedback from others about whether I've become more compassionate

The Idea in Brief

Life's a zero-sum game, right? The more you strive to win in one dimension (e.g., your work), the more the other three dimensions (your self, your home, and your community) must lose. Not according to Friedman. You don't have to make trade-offs among life's domains. Nor should you:

trading off can leave you feeling exhausted, unfulfilled, or isolated. And it hurts the people you care about most.

To excel in all dimensions of life, use Friedman's Total Leadership process. First, articulate who and what matters most in your life. Then experiment with small changes that enhance your satisfaction and performance in *all four domains*. For example, exercising three mornings a week gives you more energy for work and improves your self-esteem and health, which makes you a better parent and friend. Friedman's research suggests that people who focus on the concept of Total Leadership have a 20%–39% increase in satisfaction in all life domains, and a 9% improvement in job performance—even while working shorter weeks.

The Idea in Practice

Total Leadership helps you mitigate a range of problems that stem from making trade-offs among the different dimensions of your life:

- Feeling unfulfilled because you're not doing what you love
- Feeling inauthentic because you're not acting according to your values
- Feeling disconnected from people who matter to you
- Feeling exhausted by trying to keep up with it all

To tackle such problems using Total Leadership, take these steps:

1. REFLECT

For each of the four domains of your life -- work, home, community, and self, reflect on how important each is to you, how much time and energy you devote to each, and how satisfied you are in each. Are there discrepancies between what is important to you and how you spend your time and energy? What is your overall life satisfaction?

2. BRAINSTORM POSSIBILITIES

Based on the insights you've achieved during your four-way reflection, brainstorm a long list of small experiments that may help you move closer to greater satisfaction in all four domains. These are new ways of doing things that would carry minimal risk and let you see results quickly. For example:

- Turning off cell phones during family dinners could help you sharpen your focus on the people who matter most to you.
- Exercising several times a week could give you more energy.
- Joining a club with coworkers could help you forge closer friendships with them.

- Preparing for the week ahead on Sunday evenings could help you sleep better and go into the new week refreshed.

3. CHOOSE EXPERIMENTS

Narrow the list of experiments you've brainstormed to the three most promising. They should:

- Improve your satisfaction and performance in all four dimensions of your life.

- Have effects viewed as positive by the people who matter to you in every dimension of your life.

- Be the most costly—in regret and missed opportunities—if you *don't* do them.

- Position you to practice skills you most want to develop and do more of what you *want* to be doing.

4. MEASURE PROGRESS

Develop a scorecard for each experiment you've chosen. For example:

Experiment: Exercise three mornings a week with spouse.

- Life Dimension Experiment's Goals

- How I Will Measure Success Implementation Steps

- Work Improved alertness and productivity

No caffeine to get through the day; more productive sales calls

- Get doctor's feedback on exercise plan.

- Join gym.

- Set alarm earlier on exercise days.

- Tell coworkers, family, and friends about my plan, how I need their help, and how it will benefit them.

- Home Increased closeness with spouse

- Fewer arguments with spouse

- Community Greater strength to participate in athletic fundraising events with friends

- Three 10K fundraising walks completed by end of year

- Self Improved self-esteem Greater confidence

CHAPTER 6

How to Play to Your Strengths

Most feedback accentuates the negative. During formal employee evaluations, discussions invariably focus on "opportunities for improvement," even if the overall evaluation is laudatory. No wonder most executives—and their direct reports—dread them.

Traditional, corrective feedback has its place, of course; every organization must filter out failing employees and ensure that everyone performs at an expected level of competence. But too much emphasis on problem areas prevents companies from reaping the best from their people. After all, it's a rare baseball player who is equally good at every position. Why should a natural third baseman labor to develop his skills as a right fielder?

This article presents a tool to help you understand and leverage your strengths. Called the Reflected Best Self (RBS) exercise, it offers a unique feedback experience that counterbalances negative input. It allows you to tap into talents you may or may not be aware of and so increase your career potential.

To begin the RBS exercise, you first need to solicit comments from family, friends, colleagues, and teachers, asking them to give specific examples of times in which those strengths were particularly beneficial. Next, you need to search for common themes in the feedback, organizing them in a table to develop a clear picture of your strong suits. Third, you must write a self-portrait—a description of yourself that summarizes and distills the accumulated information. And finally, you need to redesign your personal job description to build on what you're good at.

The RBS exercise will help you discover who you are at the top of your game. Once you're aware of your best self, you can shape the positions you choose to play both now and in the next phase of your career.

Most feedback accentuates the negative. During formal employee evaluations, discussions invariably focus on "opportunities for improvement," even if the overall evaluation is laudatory. Informally, the sting of criticism lasts longer than the balm of praise. Multiple studies have shown that people pay keen attention to negative information. For example, when asked to recall important emotional events, people remember four negative memories for every positive one. No wonder most executives give and receive performance reviews with all the enthusiasm of a child on the way to the dentist.

Traditional, corrective feedback has its place, of course; every organization must filter out failing employees and ensure that everyone performs at an expected level of competence. Unfortunately, feedback that ferrets out flaws can lead otherwise talented managers to overinvest in shoring up or papering over their perceived weaknesses, or forcing themselves onto an ill-fitting template. Ironically, such a focus on problem areas prevents companies from reaping the best performance from its people. After all, it's a rare baseball player who is equally good at every position. Why should a natural third baseman labor to develop his skills as a right fielder?

Why should a natural third baseman labor to develop his skills as a right fielder?

The alternative, as the Gallup Organization researchers Marcus Buckingham, Donald Clifton, and others have suggested, is to foster excellence in the third baseman by identifying and harnessing his unique strengths. It is a paradox of human psychology that while people remember criticism, they respond to praise. The former makes them defensive and therefore unlikely to change, while the latter produces confidence and the desire to perform better. Managers who build up their strengths can reach their highest potential. This positive approach does not pretend to ignore or deny the problems that traditional feedback mechanisms identify. Rather, it offers a separate and unique feedback experience that counterbalances negative input. It allows managers to tap into strengths they may or may not be aware of and so contribute more to their organizations.

During the past few years, we have developed a powerful tool to help people understand and leverage their individual talents. Called the Reflected Best Self (RBS) exercise, our method allows managers to develop a sense of their "personal best" in order to increase their future potential. The RBS exercise is but one example of new approaches springing from an area of research called positive organizational scholarship (POS). Just as psychologists know that people respond better to praise than to criticism, organizational behavior scholars are finding that when companies focus on positive attributes such as resilience and trust, they can reap impressive bottom-line returns. (For more on this research, see the sidebar "The Positive Organization.") Thousands of executives, as well as tomorrow's leaders enrolled in business schools around the world, have completed the RBS exercise.

The Positive Organization

Positive organizational scholarship (POS) is an area of organizational behavior research that focuses on the positive dynamics (such as strength, resilience, vitality, trust, and so on) that lead to positive effects (like improved productivity and performance) in individuals and organizations. The word "positive" refers to the discipline's affirmative bias, "organizational" focuses on the processes and conditions that occur in group contexts, and "scholarship" reflects the rigor, theory, scientific procedures, and precise definition in which the approach is grounded.

The premise of POS research is that by understanding the drivers of positive behavior in the workplace, organizations can rise to new levels of achievement. For example, research by Marcial Losada and Emily Heaphy at the University of Michigan suggests that when individuals or teams hear five positive comments to every negative one, they unleash a level of positive energy that fuels higher levels of individual and group performance. Kim Cameron, a POS researcher, has demonstrated how this positive approach has helped the workers at Rocky Flats, a nuclear site in Colorado, tackle difficult and dangerous work in record time. Begun in 1995 and estimated to take 70 years and $36 billion, the Rocky Flats cleanup project is now slated for completion in ten years, with a price tag of less than $7 billion. Kaiser-Hill, the company in charge of the cleanup, replaced a culture of denial with one that fostered employee flexibility and celebrated achievements. The result was that employees developed new procedures that were fast, smart, and safe.

POS does not adopt one particular theory or framework but draws from the full spectrum of organizational theories to explain and predict high performance. To that end, a core part of the POS mission is to create cases, tools, and assessments that can help organizations improve their practices. The Reflected Best Self exercise is just one example of the kinds of practice tools available from POS. (For more information about POS, see the University of Michigan's Web site at www.bus.umich.edu/positive/.)

In this article, we will walk you through the RBS exercise step-by-step and describe the insights and results it can yield. Before we proceed, however, a few caveats are in order. First, understand that the tool is not designed to stroke your ego; its purpose is to assist you in developing a plan for more effective action. (Without such a plan, you'll keep running in place.) Second, the lessons generated from the RBS exercise can elude you if you don't pay sincere attention to them. If you are too burdened by time pressures and job demands, you may just file the information away and forget about it. To be effective, the exercise requires commitment, diligence, and follow-through. It may even be helpful to have a coach keep you on task. Third, it's important to conduct the RBS exercise at a different time of year than the traditional performance review so that negative feedback from traditional mechanisms doesn't interfere with the results of the exercise.

Used correctly, the RBS exercise can help you tap into unrecognized and unexplored areas of potential. Armed with a constructive, systematic process for gathering and analyzing data about your best self, you can burnish your performance at work.

Step 1: Identify Respondents and Ask for Feedback

The first task in the exercise is to collect feedback from a variety of people inside and outside work. By gathering input from a variety of sources—family members, past and present colleagues, friends, teachers, and so on—you can develop a much broader and richer understanding of yourself than you can from a standard performance evaluation.

As we describe the process of the Reflected Best Self exercise, we will highlight the experience of Robert Duggan (not his real name), whose self-discovery process is typical of the managers we've observed. Having retired from a successful career in the military at a fairly young age and earned an MBA from a top business school, Robert accepted a midlevel management position at an IT services firm. Despite strong credentials and leadership experience, Robert remained stuck in the same position year after year. His performance evaluations were generally good but not strong enough to put him on the high-potential track. Disengaged, frustrated, and disheartened, Robert grew increasingly stressed and disillusioned with his company. His workday felt more and more like an episode of *Survivor*.

Seeking to improve his performance, Robert enrolled in an executive education program and took the RBS exercise. As part of the exercise, Robert gathered feedback from 11 individuals from his past and present who knew him well. He selected a diverse but balanced group—his wife and two other family members, two friends from his MBA program, two colleagues from his time in the army, and four current colleagues.

Robert then asked these individuals to provide information about his strengths, accompanied by specific examples of moments when Robert used those strengths in ways that were meaningful to them, to their families or teams, or to their organizations. Many people—Robert among them—feel uncomfortable asking for exclusively positive feedback, particularly from colleagues. Accustomed to hearing about their strengths and weaknesses simultaneously, many executives imagine any positive feedback will be unrealistic, even false. Some also worry that respondents might construe the request as presumptuous or egotistical. But once managers accept that the exercise will help them improve their performance, they tend to dive in.

Within ten days, Robert received e-mail responses from all 11 people describing specific instances when he had made important contributions—including pushing for high quality under a tight deadline, being inclusive in communicating with a diverse group, and digging for critical information. The answers he received surprised him. As a military veteran and a technical person holding an MBA, Robert rarely yielded to his emotions. But in reading story after story from his respondents, Robert found himself deeply moved as if he were listening to appreciative speeches at a party thrown in his honor. The stories were also surprisingly convincing. He had more strengths than he knew.

Gathering Feedback

A critical step in the Reflected Best Self exercise involves soliciting feedback from family, friends, teachers, and colleagues. E-mail is an effective way of doing this, not only because it's comfortable and fast but also because it's easy to cut and paste responses into an analysis table such as the one in the main body of this article.

Below is the feedback Robert, a manager we observed, received from a current colleague and from a former coworker in the army.

From: Amy Chen

To: Robert Duggan

Subject: Re: Request for feedback

Dear Robert,

One of the greatest ways that you add value is that you stand for doing the right thing. For example, I think of the time that we were behind on a project for a major client and quality began to slip. You called a meeting and suggested that we had a choice: We could either pull a C by satisfying the basic requirements, or we could pull an A by doing excellent work. You reminded us that we could contribute to a better outcome. In the end, we met our deadline, and the client was very happy with the result.

From: Mike Bruno

To: Robert Duggan

Subject: Re: Request for feedback

One of the greatest ways you add value is that you persist in the face of adversity. I remember the time that we were both leading troops under tight security. We were getting conflicting information from the ground and from headquarters. You pushed to get the ground and HQ folks to talk to each other despite the tight time pressure. That information saved all of our lives. You never lost your calm, and you never stopped expecting or demanding the best from everyone involved.

Step 2: Recognize Patterns

In this step, Robert searched for common themes among the feedback, adding to the examples with observations of his own, then organizing all the input into a table. (To view parts of Robert's table, see the exhibit "Finding Common Themes.") Like many who participate in the RBS exercise, Robert expected that, given the diversity of respondents, the comments he received would be inconsistent or even competing. Instead, he was struck by their uniformity. The comments from his wife and family members were similar to those from his army buddies and work colleagues. Everyone took note of Robert's courage under pressure, high ethical standards, perseverance, curiosity, adaptability, respect for diversity, and team-building skills. Robert suddenly realized that even his small, unconscious behaviors had made a huge impression on others. In many cases, he had forgotten about the specific examples cited until he read the feedback, because his behavior in those situations had felt like second nature to him.

Finding Common Themes

The RBS exercise confirmed Robert's sense of himself, but for those who are unaware of their strengths, the exercise can be truly illuminating. Edward, for example, was a recently minted MBA executive in an automotive firm. His colleagues and subordinates were older and more experienced than he, and he felt uncomfortable disagreeing with them. But he learned through the RBS exercise that his peers appreciated his candid alternative views and respected the diplomatic and respectful manner with which he made his assertions. As a result, Edward grew bolder in making the case for his ideas, knowing that his boss and colleagues listened to him, learned from him, and appreciated what he had to say.

Other times, the RBS exercise sheds a more nuanced light on the skills one takes for granted. Beth, for example, was a lawyer who negotiated on behalf of nonprofit organizations. Throughout her life, Beth had been told she was a good listener, but her exercise respondents noted that the interactive, empathetic, and insightful manner in which she listened made her particularly effective. The specificity of the feedback encouraged Beth to take the lead in future negotiations that required delicate and diplomatic communications.

For naturally analytical people, the analysis portion of the exercise serves both to integrate the feedback and develop a larger picture of their capabilities. Janet, an engineer, thought she could study her feedback as she would a technical drawing of a suspension bridge. She saw her "reflected best self" as something to interrogate and improve. But as she read the remarks from family, friends, and colleagues, she saw herself in a broader and more human context. Over time, the stories she read about her enthusiasm and love of design helped her rethink her career path toward more managerial roles in which she might lead and motivate others.

Step 3: Compose Your Self-Portrait

The next step is to write a description of yourself that summarizes and distills the accumulated information. The description should weave themes from the feedback together with your self-observations into a composite of who you are at your best. The self-portrait is not designed to be a complete psychological and cognitive profile. Rather, it should be an insightful image that you can use as a reminder of your previous contributions and as a guide for future action. The portrait itself should not be a set of bullet points but rather a prose composition beginning with the phrase, "When I am at my best, I…" The process of writing out a two- to four-paragraph narrative cements the image of your best self in your consciousness. The narrative form also helps you draw connections between the themes in your life that may previously have seemed disjointed or unrelated. Composing the portrait takes time and demands careful consideration, but at the end of this process, you should come away with a rejuvenated image of who you are.

In developing his self-portrait, Robert drew on the actual words that others used to describe him, rounding out the picture with his own sense of himself at his best. He excised competencies that felt off the mark. This didn't mean he discounted them, but he wanted to assure that the overall portrait felt authentic and powerful. "When I am at my best," Robert wrote, I stand by my values and can get others to understand why doing so is important. I choose the harder right over the easier wrong. I enjoy setting an example. When I am in learning mode and am curious and passionate about a project, I can work intensely and untiringly. I enjoy taking things on that others might be afraid of or see as too difficult. I'm able to set limits and find alternatives when a current approach is not working. I don't always assume that I am right or know best, which engenders respect from others. I try to empower and give credit to others. I am tolerant and open to differences.

As Robert developed his portrait, he began to understand why he hadn't performed his best at work: He lacked a sense of mission. In the army, he drew satisfaction from the knowledge that the safety of the men and women he led, as well as the nation he served, depended on the quality of his work. He enjoyed the sense of teamwork and variety of problems to be solved. But as an IT manager in charge of routine maintenance on new hardware products, he felt bored and isolated from other people.

The portrait-writing process also helped Robert create a more vivid and elaborate sense of what psychologists would call his "possible self"—not just the person he is in his day-to-day job but the person he might be in completely different contexts. Organizational researchers have shown that when we develop a sense of our best possible self, we are better able make positive changes in our lives.

Step 4: Redesign Your Job

Having pinpointed his strengths, Robert's next step was to redesign his personal job description to build on what he was good at. Given the fact that routine maintenance work left him cold, Robert's challenge was to create a better fit between his work and his best self. Like most RBS participants, Robert found that the strengths the exercise identified could be put into play in his current position. This involved making small changes in the way he worked, in the composition of his team, and in the way he spent his time. (Most jobs have degrees of freedom in all three of these areas; the trick is operating within the fixed constraints of your job to redesign work at the margins, allowing you to better play to your strengths.)

Robert began by scheduling meetings with systems designers and engineers who told him they were having trouble getting timely information flowing between their groups and Robert's maintenance team. If communication improved, Robert believed, new products would not continue to be saddled with the serious and costly maintenance issues seen in the past. Armed with a carefully documented history of those maintenance problems as well as a new understanding of his naturally analytical and creative team-building skills, Robert began meeting regularly with the designers and engineers to brainstorm better ways to prevent problems with new products. The meetings satisfied two of Robert's deepest best-self needs: He was interacting with more people at work, and he was actively learning about systems design and engineering.

Robert's efforts did not go unnoticed. Key executives remarked on his initiative and his ability to collaborate across functions, as well as on the critical role he played in making new products more reliable. They also saw how he gave credit to others. In less than nine months, Robert's hard work paid off, and he was promoted to program manager. In addition to receiving more pay and higher visibility, Robert enjoyed his work more. His passion was reignited; he felt intensely alive and authentic. Whenever he felt down or lacking in energy, he reread the original e-mail feedback he had received. In difficult situations, the e-mail messages helped him feel more resilient.

Robert was able to leverage his strengths to perform better, but there are cases in which RBS findings conflict with the realities of a person's job. This was true for James, a sales executive who told us he was "in a world of hurt" over his work situation. Unable to meet his ambitious sales goals, tired of flying around the globe to fight fires, his family life on the verge of collapse, James had suffered enough. The RBS exercise revealed that James was at his best when managing people and leading change, but these natural skills did not and could not come into play in his current job. Not long after he did the exercise, he quit his high-stress position and started his own successful company.

Other times, the findings help managers aim for undreamed-of positions in their own organizations. Sarah, a high-level administrator at a university, shared her best-self portrait with key colleagues, asking them to help her identify ways to better exploit her strengths and talents. They suggested that she would be an ideal candidate for a new executive position. Previously, she would never have considered applying for the job, believing herself unqualified. To her surprise, she handily beat out the other candidates.

Beyond Good Enough

We have noted that while people remember criticism, awareness of faults doesn't necessarily translate into better performance. Based on that understanding, the RBS exercise helps you remember your strengths—and construct a plan to build on them. Knowing your strengths also offers you a better understanding of how to deal with your weaknesses—and helps you gain the confidence you need to address them. It allows you to say, "I'm great at leading but lousy at numbers. So rather than teach me remedial math, get me a good finance partner." It also allows you to be clearer in addressing your areas of weakness as a manager. When Tim, a financial services executive, received feedback that he was a great listener and coach, he also became more aware that he had a tendency to spend too much time being a cheerleader and too little time keeping his employees to task. Susan, a senior advertising executive, had the opposite problem: While her feedback lauded her results-oriented management approach, she wanted to be sure that she hadn't missed opportunities to give her employees the space to learn and make mistakes.

In the end, the strength-based orientation of the RBS exercise helps you get past the "good enough" bar. Once you discover who you are at the top of your game, you can use your strengths to better shape the positions you choose to play—both now and in the next phase of your career.

CHAPTER 7

Get Ready for Your Next Assignment

Your next internal assignment is your next chance to create results—for your organization and for your career—and a smart investment of time and effort up front can mark the difference between getting by and truly excelling. A key factor in your transition will be knowledge—not only substantive information about the project or field, but an understanding of how others inside and outside the organization have tackled similar assignments, what challenges and opportunities lie ahead, what resources are available, and how to mobilize those resources to overcome any obstacles you may encounter. The authors provide practical steps that will help you not only get smart for your next assignment but also stay smart, building knowledge capital to excel in new roles throughout your career. They then expand on those steps, which they call *phase zero, learning tour,* and *affinity groups.*

When Bruce Wilkinson, an executive in World Vision International's Zambia operation, learned that he was going to be promoted to regional director for southern Africa, he immediately started reading performance reviews of key staff members and talking to his peers, other national officers in the $2.6 billion organization. In doing so he uncovered a serious weakness: A host of critical positions in the region had gone unfilled for as long as 16 months, leading to lost contracts and deterioration in the programs WVI undertakes to empower poor communities. Human resources needed to step up its game.

But Wilkinson also saw that his appointment offered an opportunity—to both fix broken functions, such as HR, and create new ones, such as quality assurance, that could improve his region's performance. He developed a plan of action that would involve laying off the top two tiers of managers—about 20 people—and asking them to reapply for their jobs. "You want the elements of your vision to take shape before you start," Wilkinson explains. "In my case, I was redefining the role of the regional office as a true service center, and managers got the message."

Most executives know what their next project or promotion will be well before the day it starts, but too few take advantage of their insider status and the time beforehand to prepare well. That is an opportunity lost.

Your next assignment is your next chance to create results—for your organization and for your career. A smart investment of time and effort up front can make the difference between simply getting by and truly excelling, between a dead-end move and a stepping-stone to bigger and better things.

A key factor in your transition will be knowledge—not only substantive information about the project or field, but an understanding of how others inside and outside the organization have tackled similar assignments, what challenges and opportunities lie ahead, and what resources are available and how you can mobilize them to overcome obstacles. Combining insights from our ongoing study of how knowledge is best captured and shared, our experience with consulting and executive search clients, and interviews with successful leaders across different types of enterprises, this article identifies three practical steps for building your knowledge capital to excel in new roles throughout your career. We call them *phase zero, learning tour,* and *affinity groups*.

Wilkinson used all three to implement his plan, reinterviewing staff members and translating his network of former peers—the national directors—into a source of feedback. This enabled him to upgrade the HR leadership, add a director of quality, and rapidly fill open positions. Let's look at each step in detail.

Phase Zero

This is a chance to use your insider advantage to become familiar with a new unit's people and performance and to discern the opportunities and challenges of your assignment—before it begins or is even announced. In the weeks leading up to the assignment, carve out and hold sacred at least 30 minutes a day to prepare. You may find ways to increase effectiveness, reduce costs, or even reassess a business model. In phase zero you can identify problems and develop a hypothesis for how to solve them—as Wilkinson did in southern Africa. And your solutions can be tested and adjusted as you move into your new role.

Among the likeliest places to look for objective data in this step are company documents—such as performance reviews and reports on services and operations—and feedback from customers and suppliers. For qualitative input, turn to colleagues who have supervised the role, interacted with it, or previously filled a similar role. Push to understand the story behind the story—for example, ask "What challenges might I encounter that aren't apparent from the description of the assignment?" Finding these people and getting the information you need, without fanfare, will help you understand expectations and possibilities, think through a plan of action, and prepare personally for the transition.

Consider the experience of Todd Hoddick, who in early 2011 became vice president of the North American entertainment division of Barco, a global visual solutions company based in Belgium, in January 2011. Having joined the firm in 2008 as vice president of digital cinema in North America,

Hoddick had developed a strong reputation for building a profitable single-business unit. In 2010 he was approached for the new position, which would add rental and staging, digital signage, home cinema, image processing, and corporate audiovisuals to his plate.

It would be a big leap. "I wanted to understand the challenges of the role I was about to assume compared with what I was already handling," Hoddick told us. He began gathering information from a colleague then in the role who would be moving to another position, as yet unannounced. "He and I were in similar strategic meetings for the company, so I was able to ask questions about the business without seeming odd," Hoddick said. He learned, for example, that the division had significantly streamlined the sales force while maintaining ambitious revenue targets.

His next stop was Barco's worldwide head of sales, to whom he would be reporting. Hoddick had one pressing query: "What constitutes success, and what do you expect me to accomplish that others haven't been able to?" The answer: "Help Barco to be the number one projection company in the world." That clearly meant more travel and some long hours up front. So Hoddick spent time preparing his family for the change and getting their support for his additional responsibilities.

Six Mistakes to Avoid in Your Next Move

1. Defining success but forgetting to identify the people who will help you get there

2. Failing to identify the true questions, problems, and roadblocks to be addressed, which may be quite different from what you assumed

3. Dominating conversations as you introduce yourself and your plan; if you speak for more than 30% of a meeting, you are hearing but not listening

4. Letting perspectives you've heard before you start overly affect your views

5. Relying on old power dynamics, which may have shifted with the new role

6. Focusing too narrowly rather than incorporating diverse perspectives

Learning Tour

Phase zero involves solitary study and under-the-radar conversations. The learning tour involves systematic dialogue with the people who can help you do your new job, including direct reports, suppliers, and customers. You'll be testing your definitions of problems and your hypotheses for solving them, identifying leverage points, building relationships, and tapping into diverse perspectives to help you understand how to energize support and convert opposition.

Hoddick's learning tour started with a big meeting in Austin, Texas, where he asked key salespeople what they needed to be successful. The answer was less paperwork and a specific back-office resource: a jack-of-all-trades named Carlos who had been laid off during the recent retrenchment. Hoddick told them that he would fix both problems if the reduced sales force would commit to hitting its numbers. Six months later the group was ahead of plan.

You should use your change of role as an excuse to meet with all the important stakeholders—even those you already know. But remember that your "first 90 days" will differ from those of an external hire, because both your reputation and your biases are established. We recommend two tactics for making the most of this step: Be mindful of your reputation in the organization, reinforcing your positive attributes and acknowledging where you will need help. And approach your team members and their ideas with an open mind. Ask inclusive, open-ended questions, such as "If you could make one change in this area tomorrow, what would it be?"

Gary Chapman took a learning tour in early 2011, when he was promoted from vice president of field operations to executive vice president of the national network at Communities in Schools—a $225 million nonprofit singled out by the White House as one of the most effective youth mentoring organizations in the nation. "I had two sides to my new team," Chapman recalls. "Field operations, where I had worked before, and research and evaluation [R&E, which audits field operations]. I had a lot of work to do to understand the latter." Right away he met with staff members to learn about their responsibilities and what motivated them. "A number of people told me there was a disconnect," he says. Audit teams worried that field teams weren't learning from their research, and field teams thought they weren't getting enough feedback and felt too busy to elicit it themselves. Although Chapman came from the field, he listened to both sides as an honest broker. He decided to introduce weekly meetings between field and R&E directors in an effort to promote collaboration.

He also reached out to the four other members of CIS's executive team and realized that he could work more closely with communications, government relations, and the development team on advocacy and fundraising. "These teams needed more information on certain groups of students so that they could make our case on the Hill, with the right data at the right time, and plug us into education dollars we hadn't accessed in the past," Chapman says. He encouraged his field and audit staffs to engage with those colleagues as well—in effect taking his unit on a learning tour of the organization and giving everyone a chance to participate in change with an open mind.

Affinity Groups

Chapman's initial check-in with other leaders on the executive team led to ongoing relationships that made him part of an internal network of influencers he hadn't been able to reach in his prior position. Finding and staying in touch with colleagues who can sharpen your thinking and connect your role to your organization's broader mission is essential not only to getting smart but also to staying smart in your new job. Many managers tap existing peer networks to share experiences, or get assigned to a working group on a specific initiative. But too few intentionally construct and hone support networks that will help them garner the skills and fresh ideas they need to succeed.

Two mind-sets can help you get the expertise and perspectives necessary for your new role: Be open to the idea that the affinity group you're looking for may not exist—and if it doesn't, then create it, either formally or informally. And recognize that the right affinity group at the start of an assignment may not be the right one over time; be willing to make changes to the composition of your internal network. Rather than asking yourself "Who can help me get this done?" as you did in your learning tour, continually ask "Whose perspectives will keep me on the right footing to advance my organization's mission, and how can I connect with those people?" Your answers may lead you to other unit heads, former leaders, or even the board.

That's exactly the question Austin Rothbard asked when he moved from vice president of strategy and business development for bowling and billiards at the leisure equipment company Brunswick to president of its Cabo Yachts division, which makes premium boats for sport fishing. His answer—after pre-assignment preparation that included fishing trips, dealer visits, and a switch from business attire to khakis and boat shoes—was to become familiar with dealer networks and create ties to the two founders of the business, who had sold it to Brunswick and were three weeks from the end of their contractual obligations. Staying in touch with those two men was critical, because dealers had great respect for them and because they continued to be innovative and bold. "As long as I could keep the founders involved," Rothbard says, "especially since I was limited in what I understood, we were able to build the best boat in the business."

Rothbard also connected regularly with the chief financial officer and the vice president for HR of Cabo's sister company, Hatteras. They gave him advice about financial and personnel decisions at Cabo. "They were extremely willing to help me understand the business and make decisions about handling challenging employees," he says. "They helped me grow as a leader."

In a very different enterprise—Maine Medical Center, in Portland—Peter Bates, newly promoted to chief medical officer, built an affinity group of senior administrators, including the CEO and the board, and tapped their wisdom for a project that represented a huge bet for MMC: developing a medical school to strengthen the hospital's talent pipeline.

"I had to understand the board's needs and interests and ground the vision in a progression of strategies that people could agree to," Bates told us. Ultimately, the CEO and key directors became passionate advocates, and the vision resulted in a partnership with the Tufts University School of Medicine, in Boston, to build a branch campus at MMC. Bates also helped create a network of community hospitals, which provide innovative educational experiences for medical students, including up to nine months in a rural facility during the third year. Throughout, he has continued to see patients, which keeps him connected to the front line. "I still practice one day a week," Bates said. "Others see that I'm not just a guy in a suit. I walk through the hospital and make myself accessible."

Phase zero, learning tours, and affinity groups can help any manager prepare for the next promotion and keep learning and growing in the job. Sometimes the steps neatly follow this sequence, and sometimes they don't. An existing affinity group may inform your approach to phase zero, for example, or an inflection point in the job may become a good excuse to take a renewed learning tour. Whatever their order, these steps are critical for role changers who want to have greater impact in their organizations— and greater success in their careers.

CHAPTER 8

Five Strategies of Successful Part-Time Work

Most professionals start working part-time to create solutions in their lives. They have young children, want to get MBAs, need to care for aging parents. All too often, though, part-time work creates as many problems as it solves. In the best-case scenario, many part-timers end up working more hours than they intended. In the worst case, they see their importance to their organizations slowly but surely fade away. Now, though, after two generations have wrestled with such arrangements, some part-time professionals have found strategies that are succeeding.

Notice that we say the part-time professionals themselves have found these solutions. For even though most executives would agree, at this point, that part-time work can benefit an organization, it's still up to the part-timers to do most of the heavy lifting. That's true for two reasons. The first is simple: overload. Making a part-time arrangement work takes time, energy, and creativity. Most executives, stressed already with too many day-to-day challenges to list here, see the design and maintenance of part-time work arrangements as just one more hassle. Second, most organizations give executives little in the way of guidelines or policies to help them manage part-time work. So managers have little incentive to get involved. Part-time professionals, then, are on their own in relatively uncharted territory. And, inevitably, mapmaking falls to the explorers themselves.

For the past two years, we have investigated part-time work as part of a wide-ranging research project examining issues surrounding work-life balance in the United States and Canada. We interviewed 30 part-time professionals in eight organizations, large and small, as well as 27 of their colleagues and managers. Our sample included engineers, financial analysts, information technology specialists, and consultants, among others. About 80% of the part-timers we spoke to were female, largely because so much of part-time work is driven by child care issues, which most often affect women.

Our research revealed strong commonalities in the approaches of successful part-time professionals. Specifically they

- make their work-life priorities, schedules, and (if possible) plans for the future transparent to the organization;

- broadcast the business cases for their arrangements and the nondisruptive—even positive—impact on results;

- establish routines to protect their time at work and rituals to protect their time at home;

- cultivate champions in senior management who not only protect them from skeptics but actively advocate for their arrangements up and down the ranks;

- gently but firmly remind their colleagues that, despite their part-time status, they're still in the game and cannot be ignored.

At first read, some of these strategies may sound familiar—they are, you may be thinking, the same tactics successful full-time professionals use to balance the demands of work and personal life. But look again. The means may be similar, but the end is different. Part-timers use these strategies to generate a protective environment. They're seeking to reduce resentment from full-time colleagues, which can result in marginalization. They're trying to decrease the ambiguity that may confuse their managers, colleagues, families—and sometimes even themselves. And they're aiming to make the organization more comfortable with the concept of part-time work. In the following pages, we'll take a look at these strategies in action. But first, a few words on what our research revealed about the general state of part-time professionals in business today.

The Part-Timer's Lot

Although nearly 10% of the professional labor force now works part-time, our research found that most part-time jobs are still based on informal agreements. Created on the fly by the part-timers and their bosses, these arrangements are continually adjusted to match the changing demands of work (such as a major client presentation) and home (a child's bout with the flu, say). When organizations do have formal policies about such benefits for part-timers as vacation time and sick pay, they usually serve as rough guidelines only. We found that even in the same company different part-time professionals could work under different terms concerning hours, pay, and benefits. In one department of an organization we studied, for instance, mothers returning from maternity leave were routinely granted part-time positions. In a unit two floors up, such an arrangement was unheard of. "Not even on the docket for discussion," was how one manager put it.

What's more, our research revealed, many part-time professionals feel that neither their colleagues nor the organization respects them. Many part-timers told us they took a lot of jibes about their assumed lack of commitment to work and about their "privileges," such as leaving early. And while most part-timers typically dismissed the razzing as a minor annoyance, they said some discrimination felt very real. Some, for example, were housed in their organization's "low-rent" district where, unlike other professionals, they shared office space with other part-timers. And most lost their eligibility to share in the year-end bonus pool. As one part-time financial analyst put it: "You'd really have to stand on your head, I think, to beat someone for a bonus who is full-time. 'You're part-time,' they say, 'so how could you possibly achieve beyond expectations?' But if I exceed expectations in the days that I'm here, then I should be just as eligible for a bonus as any full-timer."

Many part-time professionals feel that neither their colleagues nor the organization respects them.

Most part-timers told us they accepted the consequences of their status as part of the deal. But they also said that sometimes their confidence was eroded, and they questioned whether the arrangement was worth the effort. "Whenever someone questions my position, it sparks a thousand questions in my mind," said a director of client accounts at a worldwide public relations firm. "Am I adding as much value as everybody else? Am I learning the high-tech stuff quickly enough when I am away so often?" Such feelings of inadequacy, some part-timers revealed, can bleed into their personal lives. As the same woman added, "When I'm at work and it seems so hard to pull off a part-time job, I wonder, 'Is my daughter happy when I'm not at home?'"

Perceived discrimination, we found, makes many part-timers feel defensive about their status, which can put them on the offensive. One executive we interviewed didn't even tell her clients that she worked part-time. "I was worried they'd think I wasn't committed or wouldn't get the work done. So if a meeting came up on a Thursday or Friday, I'd be there or I'd send someone for me. I was always accessible by phone and e-mail." Another part-timer told us she had become so defensive about her status that she took steps at work that ultimately undermined the very flexibility she sought from her part-time arrangement. If special training was offered on her day off, for instance, she'd still attend, or if a child was ill on the day of a big meeting, she'd still send him to school. When a big project was due, she'd work nights and weekends. "It's worth it," she told us, "so the organization knows I am as committed to them as they are to me."(Incidentally, this woman was not part of the group of part-time professionals from which we drew our conclusions about successful strategies.)

Perceived discrimination makes many part-timers feel defensive about their status, which can put them on the offensive.

These stories are extreme cases. But nearly all of our respondents admitted that work regularly crept into the private areas of their lives. Study participants typically encouraged emergency calls at home, attended important meetings during their scheduled time off, and used technology to stay in touch with work. True, these practices were usually described as exceptions, but they happened often enough to suggest that the boundary between work and home is difficult to protect.

Fortunately, the picture for part-time professionals is not entirely grim—far from it. Let's take a look at the strategies that part-timers have devised to make their unique status a success.

Strategy 1: Successful part-time professionals make their work-life priorities, schedules, and (if possible) plans for the future transparent to the organization.

Although the majority of part-time professionals are women seeking more time with their children, the reasons for alternative work arrangements vary as much as the professionals themselves. Some individuals in our study worked part-time in order to go back to school; others were caring for aging parents. It's precisely because part-time professionals have such diverse motives that they need to be frank about their priorities. Such clarity paves the way for the open, honest communication on which part-time work thrives.

Would-be part-timers cannot assume their employers will automatically divine the reasons for moving to part-time status. Many bosses will shy away from knowing anything about an employee's private life in a well-intentioned effort to respect her privacy. But not knowing the part-timer's "life story," so to speak, has its consequences. A number of managers and coworkers in our study, for instance, were remarkably reluctant to contact part-timers at home. Ironically, this usually added to the part-time professionals' workloads: once back in the office, they had to correct festering problems that could easily have been resolved through a quick call.

The most successful part-timers in our study avoided such land mines by clearly explaining to bosses and colleagues why they were working part-time, what kinds of intrusions on their home time were acceptable, and even how long they planned to stay part-time. In short, they were explicit about their priorities. One successful part-time professional, for instance, announced in writing to a wide swath of her coworkers that she was working part-time so that she could be with her young daughter in the afternoons but that she still considered her work central to her life and looked forward to returning to working full-time in 18 months. Another woman made her priorities explicit, saying she was working 20 hours a week because she had entered an eight- to ten-year time in her life when her family came first, period. These two approaches to part-time work imply two very different relationships between the part-timer and the organization. Both can succeed, however, because they are perfectly clear.

Counsel for Managers

Many managers are not enthusiastic about supporting part-time professionals. Indeed, part-time work may not suit your company. Even in the best of situations, the transition from full-time to part-time is difficult, and managers need to carefully evaluate potential part-timers. As a manager in a telecommunications company put it, "It's a hard road for me and for the employee. I wouldn't do this for just anyone." In fact, our research shows that the odds of success go way up if managers look for people who have already demonstrated success in a full-time position. In addition, this individual should fiercely want a part-time position and have a palpable reason for making it work.

Adding part-time professionals to the staff definitely complicates a manager's life. Suddenly you are called on to determine what constitutes a "fair" schedule and workload. Don't count on guidelines—there aren't any. And it doesn't end there. How are you going to evaluate your part-timer when it comes to bonuses? Is it possible to assess performance for the entire staff in a uniform way, or will the part-timer require more sensitive arrangements? In addition to these concerns, managers also have to work closely with all the people the part-timer interacts with. Sure, it's up to the part-timer to build networks with colleagues and clients, but managers constantly need to take the temperature of the experiment, especially in the early stages. How is the arrangement going for the client? For coworkers? What's life like for the part-timer? The answers to these questions may not be as straightforward as they might seem. As one oil company manager discovered: "I found out quite by chance that our part-timer was demoralized by her workload. The arrangement almost collapsed, and we came close to losing a good employee."

Once you decide to take on a part-timer, moreover, you need to recognize up front that there are limits to the arrangement. Our research suggests, for example, that part-timers are not best placed in situations that demand a lot of face-to-face time—that is, when the politics of a project are precarious or when project members require a lot of hand-holding and cajoling. There are other restrictions. "Sometimes you just don't want a part-timer in charge of a new or complex project," t he manager of one company put it bluntly.

Every part-time arrangement is unique. Having one bad—or good— experience doesn't guarantee that you'll have another like it. Every arrangement needs to be set up and managed on its own merits. Who is the particular employee? What is the specific task that needs to be done? In each case, the managerial challenge is to figure out what makes for a good part-timer—and what makes for good part-time work.

Our research showed that the more explicit employees can be about their priorities, the greater the chances are that they can sit down with their managers and shape mutually satisfying working arrangements. When part-timers clearly articulate their needs, employers can work out what degree of commitment to expect, not just at the beginning but throughout the arrangement. Consider a systems analyst for a major oil company. When he first approached his managers, he was blunt about his personal priorities: "I told them I wanted to participate more in the rearing of my children and I wanted to start my MBA. I explained that I wanted to work part-time—and, for me, that was nonnegotiable." This tough stance gave both the analyst and his management a clear understanding of what he needed as they worked together to design a feasible solution. They ended up forging an unusually favorable part-time deal for two years. The analyst would work two days a week, and the organization agreed that he would not be required to stretch his work commitments without ample notice. The analyst's project manager agreed to take up some of the slack when he, the analyst, was out of the office. The manager was prepared to step in, she explained, because the analyst had a stellar track record, and she was confident that he was making the project's success a priority.

Like the systems analyst, all the successful part-timers in our study were individuals who had formerly done outstanding full-time work. Indeed, part-time work is not a viable route for anyone who hasn't already demonstrated superiority in a traditional setting. Successful part-timers know the company ropes. They've learned the organization's rules, they've mastered those rules, and now they're ready to change them. Of course, not every part-time professional can—or wants to—set down such unequivocal terms. But making their new priorities transparent to the organization will help professionals outperform in their part-time positions just as they did when they were full-time.

Strategy 2: Successful part-time professionals broadcast the business cases for their arrangements and the nondisruptive—even positive—impact on results.

Simply put, the main reason most bosses and colleagues object to part-time work is that they suspect it will disrupt the business. They're afraid work won't get done on time or that other people, already at full capacity, will need to pick up the part-timer's unwanted assignments. These worries are legitimate. That's why the successful part-timers in our study did not ignore or gloss over them. They addressed them head on.

First, many part-timers help their organizations to see that the arrangement makes more sense than a complete departure. This always needs to be handled with subtlety, for obvious reasons. No one likes to hear, "Consider yourself lucky you've got me at all!" But there is really no reason for being so direct. Bosses know that part-timers have successful track records—as well as insider knowledge, existing relationships, and technical expertise.

They need only a slight nudge to remind them what would happen if a part-timer were to move to the competition.

Second, successful part-timers publicize the business cases for their arrangements by demonstrating that the work is still getting done, well and on time. One fundamental way they do this is by building strong alliances with their colleagues. In fact, the successful part-timers in our study involved their coworkers as much as possible in the initial transition from full-time status. One customer service engineer, for example, discussed the shift to part-time with all the members of her team before she raised the idea formally: "Politically, it would have been impossible for my boss to turn me down."

Nevertheless, a part-time arrangement will in fact change the way work gets done. In consulting businesses, for instance, with their high premium on service, the part-timer will not always be available to the client. Extra work will inevitably spill over to coworkers, causing friction among even the best-oiled groups. Therefore, successful part-timers go to great lengths to reassure colleagues that they are not simply entitled to special privileges. At times, this means reminding people that although they work less, part-timers also earn less.

At all times, it is important for part-timers to frame the extra responsibilities that fall on coworkers and subordinates as opportunities. Thus, the successful part-timer is careful to delegate work around her colleagues' development needs by, for instance, having a compatriot who needs to work on facilitation skills lead a meeting the part-timer is not going to. In this way, she can help coworkers benefit from the extra work they're given.

Finally, creating a business case for a reduced schedule often requires part-timers to redesign their work so that they, in effect, end up doing the same amount of work but more efficiently. Those part-timers we studied who were able to achieve this heightened productivity were almost always highly motivated, committed self-starters. Consider a customer service manager for a phone company. She took the job on a half-time basis. Her predecessor had held the same job full-time. The work content didn't diminish at all. In fact, it increased. But the service manager now gets the job done in half the time.

This is often the case. All the successful part-timers in our study had rich anecdotal evidence of their ability to squeeze more work into less time. And the managers interviewed in our study agreed. Said a manager of two engineers who worked part-time: "We probably get as much productivity out of our part-time professionals as we do from some of the employees who are here five days a week."

Strategy 3: Successful part-time professionals establish routines to protect their time at work and rituals to protect their time at home.

Our study showed that successful part-timers approach the pace and flow of their work in a wide variety of ways. One financial analyst at an electric utility, for instance, spread out her days in the office, working Mondays, Wednesdays, and Fridays. The benefit, she claimed, was that she stayed in touch with the work situation, and her mind was less likely to drop out of work mode. But another professional in our study—an account executive at a major oil company—stayed focused by doing just the reverse. She worked Monday through Wednesday every week.

No matter what their schedules, successful part-time professionals establish routines that are transparent to their colleagues and bosses and help them separate work and home in their own minds. From the company's perspective, we found, the nature of the routine selected is much less important than its sheer regularity. Similarly, the successful part-timers in our study demarcated home and work with personalized rituals, which again served to clarify where they were and when.

But successful part-timers don't stop at organizing their own work. They pay attention to how the work is flowing when they're not around, as well. One systems analyst, for example, described how colleagues would let work slide until Thursday because they knew she wouldn't be coming into the office until then. This led her to establish monitoring routines in which she hounded people virtually on her days off. Every day or so, she left voice-mail and e-mail messages ensuring that the flow of work continued smoothly. Communication routines let her know when she needed to put her foot down. They also let her colleagues know that she was never very far away.

Routines, of course, are easier praised than actually practiced. Business is always in flux; emergencies happen. Meetings come up unexpectedly, often throwing the airtight schedule of the part-timer into disarray. That's why in establishing their routines part-timers need to set some judicious rules about their participation in meetings.

Now it might seem logical for part-timers to attend all the meetings they can when they're in the office: after all, missing meetings on days off is already something of a political statement. It implies, " I don't care about this organization's pecking order. I come and go as I please." Few part-timers deliberately want to make such a statement. But our research suggests that a surprising number of successful part-time professionals miss meetings even on days when they are in the office, as part of their standard routine. One systems analyst we interviewed was emphatic about the need to protect her work time: "I tend to avoid meetings like the plague because they're a waste of time." In fact, successful part-timers draw on their insider knowledge of organizational routines to make tough judgment calls about which meetings they can safely ignore and which they need to attend.

Now for rituals, which are important, we found, because they fortify the boundaries between work and home that part-timers need to sustain their delicate arrangements. So one part-timer described how every week, come what may, he coaches his daughter's basketball team and attends all the games. Another part-timer who doesn't work on Fridays deliberately leaves her laptop at work on Thursday nights. Still another professional fills up her home time with piano lessons and sewing classes. " I'm not a schedule person," she said, "but I've consciously scheduled my time."

Unlike routines, rituals often have a symbolic component in that they force part-time professionals to invest not only time but also emotion into something. We heard from a number of part-timers who regularly participated in a range of community groups, from gardening clubs to dance troupes to Bible study groups. These activities demand a commitment from part-timers to people and places that are unrelated to work—and often unrelated to Children and home. These rituals that part-time professionals erect in their lives are among the most effective because they genuinely break connections with the known world and forge new ties.

Strategy 4: Successful part-time professionals cultivate champions in senior management who not only protect them from skeptics but actively advocate for their arrangements up and down the ranks.

The idiosyncratic nature of part-time work makes each part-time professional an organizational innovator, with all the risks that innovation implies. And, as with any risky investment, the part-time position often requires a sponsor, someone who can influence the way the company views the shift to part-time work. Consider the experience of an IT specialist working at a gas pipeline company. She was stressed out, losing weight, and finding it impossible to do her job while raising three children. Although her coworkers were compassionate, they couldn't see how a part-time arrangement could work out without harming them. Without some senior-level support, the IT specialist wasn't going to get anywhere. But she fought hard for a change in status. She talked to a wide range of potential champions until finally she found a sympathetic ear. Although he didn't have an immediate solution, he was able to find another person looking to go part-time. Eventually, he arranged a job they could share.

All the successful part-timers in our study had champions in senior management who helped them overcome obstacles that would otherwise have caused them to fail. That was particularly true for women coming back from maternity leave who assumed (mistakenly) that there would automatically be workable part-time jobs waiting for them when they got back. Champions also play important roles after the work arrangements have been settled. Often, they run interference with clients, managers, and colleagues who may believe that part-timers aren't holding up their end of the bargain. Champions often have to intervene with clients to protect part-timers from excessive customer demands. But champions also make sure that managers are aware of part-timers' contributions and potential so that companies consider these professionals for promotions, bonuses, and choice assignments.

Finally, champions keep part-timers in the loop. They make sure that the part-timer knows what's going on behind the scenes. One champion, for instance, warned his part-time systems analyst that he hadn't been visible enough in the past couple months: "I think you need to go and talk to your team," the champion said. "A few people are reportedly unhappy that you've been so aloof lately." Over time, a good champion accepts some responsibility for making the part-time position work, becoming the part-timer's mentor and protector.

There's no single profile of the ideal champion, but our study found them all to be highly networked change agents—individuals accustomed to using their charisma to influence people at every level of the company. They also tended to be sympathetic to the plight of part-timers because their own spouses or partners were also trying to navigate the challenges of part-time work. Their support of part-time work was, in other words, often quite personal.

Strategy 5: Successful part-time professionals gently but firmly remind their colleagues that, despite their part-time status, they're still in the game and cannot be ignored.

In addition to needing a powerful champion, the part-timer must also build a strong network of allies in the organization to avoid becoming marginalized. Unfortunately, because of their intensified work schedules, part-time professionals often focus on work to the exclusion of making small talk in the corridors. As one consultant in a public relations firm put it: "I want to stay out of politics and all the stuff that floats around. I want to focus on my job. The rest bogs me down."

Our research suggests that such behavior ultimately hurts a professional who already spends so much time away from the office. Office gossip, in particular, helps the part-timer stay tied in. In fact, staying connected turned out to be so important in our study that we've taken to defining a successful part-time professional as someone who can squander time productively at work. Consider Yvonne, the part-time financial analyst at the electric utility. She said that maintaining her social networks was one of the biggest factors in her success. "Some people say I only come in for lunch!" she said. "And I do have a lunch date almost every day that I come in. But that's how I get the informal information I need to make the part-time position work."

In addition to tuning in to gossip in these informal conversations, part-timers constantly need to emphasize what they have in common with their full-time colleagues. By saying, "I'm not so different from you," part-timers can reassure coworkers that they're not getting a special deal. Take the case of a senior auditor at the gas pipeline company, who successfully defused a coworker's envy over her attendance at a training meeting. "He came up to me and said, 'What are you doing here? Do you get paid to be trained?' 'Yes,' I gently replied. 'Every employee does.'"

The real challenge for part-timers is making their presence felt when they are so often out of the office. Interestingly, every successful part-timer in our study had some trick for staying visible in the organization despite the many hours spent away from work. Some part-timers, for example, sent voice-mails on days when they weren't in the office. Some managed their own projects—and championed others' besides—to show they were very involved. One part-timer devised an elaborate series of meetings, planned and announced long in advance. "Just in case anyone has any doubts," she said defiantly. "I'm around and intend to be for a long time." Successful part-timers show that they cannot be ignored.

Every successful part-timer in our study had some trick for staying visible in the organization despite the many hours spent away from work.

Begun more than 20 years ago, part-time professional work is an experiment that has met with mixed results. In most cases, the arrangement is an attempt to give a woman more time to raise her family. But it is not necessarily a panacea for striking a balance between work and life. Many part-timers are forced to work longer hours than they contracted for, and many suffer under the second-class status of part-time work.

At the same time, part-time work makes organizations uncomfortable. It raises obvious questions about who will pick up the slack. And it raises more fundamental questions about the very nature of professional work itself. What exactly is a professional being paid for? Time or output? When limits are placed on time and pay, how should that fairly be reflected in the work?

Successful part-timers face such difficulties head on. The five strategies we've distilled from the experience of the successful part-timers work together to overcome these challenges. They not only help the part-timer deal with the organization but also make the organization itself more receptive to the possibilities of part-time work.

CHAPTER 9

Rebounding from Career Setbacks

It's not easy to recover from a big career disappointment such as getting fired or being passed over for a promotion. Many people sink into anger or denial, blaming situational factors or company politics. Though that's a natural response, it can also prevent them from breaking free of the destructive behaviors that may have derailed them in the first place.

People who successfully rebound from career losses take a different approach: They do the hard work of figuring out why they lost, identifying which new paths they could take, and then seizing the right opportunity whether that's a different role in the same organization, a move to a new company, or a shift to a new industry or career.

Drawing on in-depth research and the authors' consulting experience, this article offers practical guidance for transforming anger and self-doubt over what seems like a failure into focused exploration and excitement about the fresh possibilities the situation presents.

To gauge your ability to rebound from career setbacks, take the self-assessment at hbr.org/assessments/mirror-test.

How well do you rebound from career setbacks? Take this self-assessment to find out.

Brian was a rising star at his company. He advanced through several senior management roles and was soon tapped to head a business unit, reporting directly to the CEO. But after about two years in the job, despite his stellar financial results, his boss suddenly dismissed him. Brian was told that the company was trying to be a more open, engaged, global enterprise and that his aggressive leadership style didn't reflect those values.

Like most ambitious managers who suffer career setbacks, Brian went through a period of shock, denial, and self-doubt. After all, he'd never previously failed in a position. He had trouble accepting the reality that he wasn't as good as he'd thought he was. He also felt upset and angry that his boss hadn't given him a chance to prove himself. Eventually, however, he recognized that he couldn't reverse the decision and chose to focus on moving forward. None of the people working for him had objected to his dismissal, so he was particularly keen to figure out how to foster loyalty in future employees.

Within a few months, a large industrial parts company impressed with Brian's undisputed ability to meet financial targets recruited him to lead a division. The job was a step down from his previous role, but he decided to take it so that he could experiment with different ways of working and

84

leading, learning to better control his emotions and rally his team around him. It paid off: Less than three years later, yet another company—this time, a *Fortune* 500 manufacturer—hired him to be its CEO. During his seven-year tenure in that job, he doubled the firm's revenue and created a culture that balanced innovation with a disciplined focus on productivity and performance.

Of course, not everyone can go from being out of a job to running a large company. But in more than 30 years of research and consulting work with executive clients, we've found that one lesson from Brian's story applies pretty universally: Even a dramatic career failure can become a springboard to success if you respond in the right way. To execute a turnaround like Brian's, you focus on a few key tasks: Determine why you lost, identify new paths, and seize the right opportunity when it's within your reach.

Figure Out Why You Lost

We've interviewed hundreds of executives who have been fired, laid off, or passed over for promotion (as a result of mergers, restructurings, competition for top jobs, or personal failings). Often, we find them working through the classic stages of loss defined by psychiatrist Elisabeth Kübler-Ross: They start with shock and denial about the events and move on to anger at the company or the boss, bargaining over their fate, and then a protracted period of licking their wounds and asking themselves whether they can ever regain the respect of their peers and team. Many of them never make it to the "acceptance" stage.

That's partly because, as social psychologists have found in decades' worth of studies, high achievers usually take too much credit for their successes and assign too much external blame for their failures. It's a type of attribution bias that protects self-esteem but also prevents learning and growth. People focus on situational factors or company politics instead of examining their own role in the problem.

Some ask others for candid feedback, but most turn to sympathetic friends, family members, and colleagues who reinforce their self-image ("You deserved that job") and feed their sense of injustice ("You have every right to be angry"). This prevents them from considering their own culpability and breaking free of the destructive behavior that derailed them in the first place. It may also lead them to ratchet back their current efforts and future expectations in the workplace.

Those who rebound from career losses take a decidedly different approach. Instead of getting stuck in grief or blame, they actively explore how they contributed to what went wrong, evaluate whether they sized up the situation correctly and reacted appropriately, and consider what they would do differently if given the chance. They also gather feedback from a wide variety of people (including superiors, peers, and subordinates), making it clear that they want honest feedback, not consolation.

Brian, for example, had to engage in frank, somewhat painful conversations with his boss, several direct reports, and a few trusted colleagues to discover that he had developed a career-limiting reputation for being difficult and not always in control of his emotions.

Also consider Stan, a senior partner at a boutique professional services firm considering global expansion. A vocal proponent of the growth plan, he had hoped to lead the company's new London office. When another partner was selected instead, Stan was outraged. He stewed for a few weeks but then resolved to take a more productive tack. He set up one-on-one meetings with members of the firm's executive committee. At the start of each session, he explained that he wasn't trying to reverse the decision; he just wanted to understand why it had been made. He took care not to sound bitter or to bad-mouth the process or the people involved. He maintained a positive, confident tone, and he expressed a willingness to learn from his missteps.

As a result, the executive committee members gave him consistent, useful comments: They regarded his aggressiveness as an asset in the United States but worried that it would get in the way of securing new clients and running an office in the UK. His initial reaction was defensive. ("No one minded my aggressiveness when it landed key contracts," he thought.) But he kept those feelings in check—and quickly came around to appreciating the candor. "It wasn't that they were asking me to change," Stan reflected, "but they made clear to me that my style got in the way of this opportunity."

Identify New Paths

The next step is to objectively weight the potential for turning your loss into a win, whether that's a different role in your organization, a move to a new company, or a shift to a different industry or career.

Reframing losses as opportunities involves hard thinking about who you are and what you want. Research shows that escapism is a common reaction to career derailment—people may take trips to get away from their troubles, immerse themselves in busywork, drink or eat excessively, or avoid discussing their thoughts and plans with family and friends. While these behaviors can give you mental space to sort things out, they rarely lead to a productive transition. It's more effective to engage in a focused exploration of all the options available.

Reframing losses as opportunities involves hard thinking about who you are and what you want.

New opportunities don't usually present themselves right away, of course, and it can be hard to spot them through the fog of anger and disappointment in the early days after a setback. Studies by change management expert William Bridges highlight the tension people feel when they're torn between hanging onto their current identities and expectations and letting go. Leaders we've counseled describe entering a "twilight zone": The status quo has been fatally disrupted, but it's not clear yet what success will look like in the future.

That's why it's useful to take time to test out some ideas for what to do next. One option is to speak with a career counselor or engage in therapy, both to clarify goals and to work on personal development. Another is to take a temporary leave from your job to go back to school or test-drive a career interest at a start-up or a nonprofit. Pausing a bit can allow you to find new meaning in your setback.

Recall how Brian reacted when he was fired from his unit-head job: He began to consider lower-level positions that would give him room to tinker with his leadership style. Or look at Paula, whom we met while studying the resiliency of online advertising executives involved in restructurings. When her high-tech company's new CEO launched a corporate makeover, Paula felt relatively safe because the European business unit she led had met or exceeded its targets for 11 straight quarters, and she had been promoted three times in five years. But then she discovered that her position would be eliminated.

At first Paula blamed everything from company politics to her boss's failure to protect her and her team. Then, three months after the announcement, her last day arrived. She had no plans and didn't want to make any right away. Instead she spent time examining her life and her career. She reached out to friends and business associates—"not to network" (her words) but to gain perspective and advice in thinking through her goals. She reflected on each conversation, made notes, and eventually developed what she dubbed "four themes for my next job": She wanted to bring new products to market (rather than relaunching U.S. offerings in other regions), to interact more directly with clients, to work for a company with a unique value proposition, and to have colleagues she liked and trusted. Paula then tailored her job search to achieve those goals.

Seize the Right Opportunity

After you identify possible next steps, it's time to pick one. Admittedly, this can be a little frightening, especially if you're venturing into unknown career territory. Reimagining your professional identity is one thing; bringing it to life is another. Remember, though, that you haven't left your skills and experience behind with your last job, and you'll also bring with you the lessons learned from the setback. You may also have productively revised your definition of success.

Research we've conducted, along with career specialist Douglas (Tim) Hall, shows that needs and priorities can change dramatically over time—as children are born or grow up and move out, after a divorce or a parent's death, when early dreams fade in midlife and new ones emerge, and when perspectives and skills become outdated and new growth challenges beckon. So choosing the right opportunity has a lot to do with the moment when you happen to be looking.

Paula's story is a case in point. Her list of "must haves" led her to interview for and accept a more senior position, as VP of international sales, at a smaller firm in the same industry. The job was located in the European city where she already lived and wanted to stay.

Brian, by contrast, took a significant step down, but he took advantage of the opportunity to learn to become a better manager. He developed an understanding of the triggers that had caused him to behave unproductively in the past and devised coping strategies. For example, instead of immediately pouncing on subordinates for performance "misses," he learned to have off-line discussions with the relevant managers. After some practice, the measured approach bgan to feel more natural to him.

Bruce, a senior IT manager at a New York bank that went through a merger, is another example. He kept his job in the deal's aftermath but was devastated to lose out in his bid to become the chief technology officer of the merged company. He stayed on through the integration, but after a year of rethinking his personal and career goals and considering a variety of jobs—he moved with his family to Austin, Texas, and joined a small technology firm that became wildly successful. Just as important, he also found time to coach his two children's soccer teams and pursue his passion for music as a guitarist for a local band.

Like Paula and Brian, Bruce did serious discovery work after his setback—and then acted with conviction. He moved to a new city, industry, and job that would allow him to recover and thrive.

For executives who decide to stay with their employers, the biggest change may be in mind-set or psychological commitment. That's what happened with Stan at the professional services firm: Having gained a clearer sense of how his colleagues viewed him, he embraced his role as rainmaker, better appreciating the income, status, and perks that came with it. He also found a new source of satisfaction and accomplishment: mentoring the next generation of talent on how to win new business.

Shifting perspective like this takes just as much energy as switching companies or jobs. If you're not able to dig into your current work with renewed gusto, as Stan did, you might decide to put more discretionary effort into family life, volunteering, or hobbies, recognizing that having a rich personal life can compensate for not being number one on your team or in your organization.We all know the importance of resilience and adaptability when it comes to career success. But these qualities don't come easily or naturally to everyone, which is why it's so useful to have clear steps to follow after a setback. The approach laid out here can help transform the anger and self-doubt associated with failure into excitement about new possibilities.

CHAPTER 10

Plan a Satisfying Retirement

You've worked hard all your life, and now you're on the brink of retirement. Trouble is, the things you looked forward to all those years — mornings on the golf course, afternoons puttering in the garden, trips to exotic places — don't feel like they'll be enough to sustain you. Encore careers — jobs that blend income, personal meaning, and often some element of giving back — are becoming an increasingly popular alternative to full-time retirement. But where do you start?

What the Experts Say

According to Encore.org, a think tank focused on Baby Boomers, work, and social purpose, nearly 9 million people ages 44 to 70 today are engaged in second-act careers. "People are leading longer and healthier lives and so leaving full-time work in your mid-60s means that you're looking at a horizon of 20 to 30 years. That's a long time," says Marc Freedman, CEO of Encore.org and the author of *The Big Shift*. There is, he says, the financial question of how you'll support yourself, "and then there is the existential question: Who you are going to be?"

On one hand, it's daunting to contemplate embarking on a new career at this stage in life. On the other hand, it's liberating to "let go of the past" and forge a new identity based on "things that you find exciting, stimulating, or interesting," says Ron Ashkenas, a senior partner at Schaffer Consulting and an executive-in-residence at UC Berkeley's Haas School of Business. "It's an opportunity to think about how you want to contribute to society, your community, and your family." Karen Dillon, coauthor of *How Will You Measure Your Life?*, agrees: "Life doesn't necessarily get simpler after you leave a full time job," she says. "But it can become more rewarding — if you're willing to hold yourself accountable and work for the new goals you've set yourself." Here are some things to think about as you prepare to for this new phase.

Lay the groundwork early

If you're confident that your job won't be in jeopardy, tell colleagues about your plans to officially retire while you're still gainfully employed. "Then it's not out of the blue, and it also gives them a chance to figure out if they have contacts or a network you could leverage," says Ashkenas. It's also important that you leave on good terms with your company and indicate if you are open to occasional projects and assignments — which is a good way to keep your hand in your profession. Adds Dillon: "You can't just stop working and expect the phone to ring. Plant seeds early so that once you're in circulation, experiences and opportunities will come to you."

Don't rush

Once you leave your job, give yourself a period of time — ideally months in duration — to reflect on what you want to do next. "Give yourself time to rest, renew, and restore," says Freedman. Navigating this transition will take some time. "You've been working and juggling family stuff for decades and likely haven't had the time to think about this next chapter of your life. Recognize that finding work that is significant and fulfilling could take two to three years."

Ask yourself: what's really important?

Make a list of all the things "that feed you emotionally" and then drill down to figure out exactly what it is about those things that inspires you and makes you happy, suggests Dillon. For instance, you might list spending time with your kids or doing work that's challenging, but "what you most enjoy is having new experiences with your children, like travel. And what you really like about work is collaborating with others and creating something," says Dillon. "Push yourself to do the things that matter to you and be conscious of the choices you're making and how you're spending your time." Your goal, says Freedman, is to "figure out what your priorities are at this juncture in your life."

Be willing to experiment

Freedman advises taking a "try-before-you-buy" approach. "Find ways to dabble in things that interest you," he says. Seek out internships, fellowships, or part-time jobs; give back by volunteering to serve on a board of a nonprofit; take on different kinds of professional assignments; or sign up for a class at a community college. "If it sounds fun and interesting and it seems as though you will learn new things, do it," says Dillon. Also look for ways to transfer your hard-earned expertise to new domains, says Ashkenas. "It's not as if you stop being who you are. You are still you, and you still have the same skills; you're just applying them to new situations and environments."

Keep productive

After you've given yourself some time off, it's important to return to some of the things that office life gave you: structure and community. "Just as you would look ahead to milestones in your work, you need things to look forward to and anticipate," Ashkenas says. Consider joining a group or community like an alumni association, a volunteer or religious organization, a freelancer's group, a book club, or even a virtual community. After all, "you need the stuff you get from the informal office environment: banter, chatter, laughter, and information," Dillon adds. It's also helpful to spend time with others who are "wrestling with the same challenges you are," says Freedman.

Hold yourself accountable

As you're navigating this transition, "you have to think about goals," says Dillon. "Get feedback from those you care about — like your spouse or partner, children, and friends — about how you're doing. And be honest with yourself about how you're spending your time. Do a reality check by asking yourself, "Do I feel good and healthy? Do I feel stimulated? Don't let outside voices dictate your answers," says Dillon. And once you figure out where you want to focus, Ashkenas says, "you need to keep asking yourself: Am I adding value? Am I making a contribution? Am I learning something?"

Principles to Remember

Do:

- Find meaning in your new life by pinpointing how you most enjoy spending your time

- Experiment with different jobs and assignments to stretch yourself and learn new things

- Expose yourself to new perspectives and ideas by joining a community

Don't:

- Be secretive about your intentions to leave your job — share your plans with colleagues and let them know you're open to new opportunities

- Rush into a new job right away; give yourself time to relax and restore

- Squander hours away just because you can; hold yourself accountable about how you're spending your time

Case study #1: Embrace your personal passions as the source of new opportunities

The day that Gail Federici sold John Frieda — the professional hair care company she co-founded with the British stylist — her mind reeled. "We hadn't been planning to sell the company," she says. "Over the years we had meetings [with prospective buyers], but we wanted to keep doing what we were doing."

Once the paperwork was signed, she took a one-week trip to Venice with her college roommate then returned home to London. At first it was a tough transition. "We had been building this company for 12 years: I had a definitive routine; I had a plan for the future; I had goals. All of a sudden it was gone," she says. Gail decided to dedicate her time and energy to a personal passion: music. It was a natural second act: Her husband is a musician and Gail used to sing in his band in New York. At the time, the couple's twin daughters were interested in becoming performers. "It was a huge learning curve for me: I had to read the back of CDs to find out the names of producers and songwriters," she says.

Over the next five years, she worked on albums and promotions with several musicians and boy bands, including Taio Cruz, the British singer-songwriter and record producer. "It was exciting and challenging to learn a new industry but I was still doing what comes easy to me: marketing, problem solving, and strategizing." After signing the main act she and her team developed to Interscope, she decided to "go back to what [she] does best."

Now in her 60s, Gail is the President and CEO of Federici Brands, another hair styling company. While she is happy to be back in the hair care business, she looks back on her years in the music industry fondly. "I was out of my comfort zone but I liked it."

Case study #2: Leverage your expertise and connections to give back

Bill Haggett spent the first part of his career in the shipbuilding business — first as President and CEO of Bath Iron Works in Maine and later as the head of Irving Shipbuilding of New Brunswick, Canada. After leaving Irving in the late 1990s and returning to Maine, Bill wanted to give back to his community.

His first priority: building a new YMCA in his hometown. Bill helped raise funds for the Y and also helped design the new complex. "I grew up in Bath, Maine in the 1940s and I am from a family of modest means," he says. "The YMCA was a terrific outlet for me and my friends."

By 2000, the Y project was complete, but Bill wasn't interested in "moving into retirement mode." The Libra Foundation, a large charitable organization in Maine, approached him about a job. "They wanted to make a strategic investment in a potato company in northern Maine on the brink of bankruptcy. And they asked: 'Would I be willing to serve as chairman and CEO?'"

Bill knew nothing about the potato business, and he had little interest in moving to northern Maine. But after reflecting on what he wanted out of the next chapter of his life, he realized the opportunity was appealing. "It was a way to help the economy by adding value and jobs in that part of the state," he says. The job would be fulfilling on a personal level too. "I wanted the challenge of turning this business around. It was a way to learn something new, but I also thought I had some expertise I could bring to the party."

The early years were a struggle, but after a while, business at Naturally Potatoes improved: Sales increased by 40%, and the company returned to profitability. By 2005, it was sold to California-based Basic America Foods (BAF). Bill, meanwhile, went on to run a meat company. But Naturally Potatoes fell short of BAF's expectations, and when, in 2010, a team led by Libra bought the company back, Bill resumed the role of CEO.

At the age of 80, Bill — who is chairman and CEO of Pineland Farms Natural Meats *and* Pineland Farms Potatoes — has no plans to stop working. "I feel energized," he says. "One of the great pleasures of being my age is that everyone I work with is younger than I am. They have bright ideas, skills, and technology savvy that I don't have." Learning a new business every few years has been "stimulating," he says. "I like to be useful and to make a contribution."

THE END

www.ingramcontent.com/pod-product-compliance
Lightning Source LLC
Chambersburg PA
CBHW070825180526
45168CB00002B/739